The Lotus Seed Life:

Struggles to Snuggles

1st Edition March 2017
V. 1

Collected by:

Victoria M. Faudel

Lotus Seed Press
Denver - London

Copyright © 2008-2017 The Lotus Seed Process, Inc.

Some names changed at the requests of the original authors.
All stories used with permission.

All rights reserved. Except as permitted under the U.S. Copyright Act of 1976, no part of this publication may be reproduced, distributed, or transmitted in any form or by any means, or stored in a database or retrieval system, without the prior written permission of the publisher.

Lotus Seed Press
9332 S. Autumn Ash Ct, Highlands Ranch, CO 80126
www.LotusSeedLife.com

ISBN-13:978-0692858011

DEDICATION

I would like to thank and acknowledge with great pride, gratitude and love:

The people in this book for the courage in sharing your stories and for giving me the opportunity to uncover the real you and watching you grow into strong beautiful empowered individuals.

The team; Gill W, Vicki W, Yvonne H, Geoff S, Tom H, Rachel W, Angela Q, Pia R, and Grace B for your commitments and dedication to helping and guiding others to achieve their dreams. Thank you for being part of my team, believing in yourselves, and for taking a stand to better this world one person at a time. Thank you for your passion, conviction, playfulness and your ability to experience life to the fullest.

To all of the past, present, and future clients and friends: Thank you for your trust, enthusiasm and the ability to embrace the changes in your mindsets and for learning your life lessons of self-control, when you would bring me your issues and I would say "I'm so happy for you," and for the fact that you have issues.

I do love each and every one of you. Every one of you is like my own child. Each one of you has touched my life and made a difference to me, and for that I am eternally grateful.

Nate, my business manager and husband, for being my biggest supporter, for answering the phone at all hours of the day and night, for all of the technical support and the countless hours of dealing with me and all my crazy ideas, for sharing my life and dreams with me, for being there to talk to me, listen to me, and to give me love and to receive mine.

God for all that I have been given; family, team, friends, clients, and all of my gifts to serve, guide and empower others, and for the opportunity to bring a little more love to the world.

Vikki

Table of Contents

Spirit's Destiny...6
Introduction..7
Vikki's Story in Her Own Words.................................8
Light at the End of the Tunnel.....................................12
My Self Worth..15
The World is My Oyster...23
My Own Voice..26
Work is Play...32
Freedom!..34
My Own Choices..40
Confidence...48
I Turned Around One Day...51
Love..52
I Know What I Want..62
My Right to Live..65
Poem: Who am I?...71
Resolving Old Conflicts...73
Forgiving to Move On..78
Run Over by a Thought Train......................................87
Sometimes Life Hits You Upside the Head.................91
Going to the Chapel...94
How I Rescued Myself...96
Fly in the Ointment..102
Finding my Pieces..104
My Onion..106
The Importance of Peanut Butter...............................107
Receiving...113
The Blind Musician...115
Conclusion...120

Spirit's Destiny

With words that only they can know

Our hearts are whispering songs of love.

Our spirits dance to haunting tunes

That only they can hear.

Our eyes see moonbeams glow and play

Rainbow colors light our way,

Our hands entwined even when apart

Destinies linked right from the start.

Our playful souls laugh and skip

In happy games where two are one.

Together always, twinned in love

This treasure found will not be lost.

Our ears hear only words of love

Echoes gently from above

Two but always of one heart

Destiny…. Right from the start.

Written by Diane Hudson

Introduction

Lotus Seed Life has touched countless people in many countries. These are their stories. These were written by people who have experienced Vikki (Founder of Lotus Seed Life) directly or through her specialists.

People with all sorts of diversity overcome all sorts of adversity. These stories are about people learning that they are better inside than anyone outside has ever seen. These are about self discovery and accomplishment. These are about people blooming to become who they are meant to be. If it is possible for them it is possible for anyone.

Vikki teaches that anything is possible if one has the right mindset. It is possible to control your mindset. It is possible to enhance your focus. It is possible to eliminate distracting and outdated beliefs. Working through life lessons can be easy. Living in the present is the answer to most fears and apprehensions.

It is my hope that this book plants some seeds of hope that things can and will be better for you than they are. Life is an opportunity to make something out of the odds and ends we are given. Each of us has so much untapped potential to live personal excellence. It is my hope that you find the path you need in order to *act* on your potential as the authors of these stories have. Contemplation and examination can bring peace of mind and action can change the world.

Living the Lotus Seed Life is a real experience. Rather than describing it I think I'll let the stories speak for themselves. We receive requests for Vikki's story on a regular basis. I'll start with that to provide some context.

Nate Faudel – Feb 22, 2017

Vikki's Story in Her Own Words

Vikki began to develop the Lotus Seed Process in 1982.

I had a few friends in a class and the question was posed 'what kind of business could we do that would be good for us and would change the world?' The class came up with a project. My friends and I kept talking. We had the ideas for wanting to help people. We were just looking for the method.

We talked for months about our ideas. One Saturday night I threw my then husband a massive birthday with all of his friends and everyone we knew. Sunday he said he was going to coffee. He came back and announced that he was divorcing me. At that moment 7 of his friends walked through the front door and they moved him out completely in about 45 minutes. They had it planned for about a week. No one told me anything at the party.

I cried for a while and went to a therapist for a while. As six months of therapy approached I asked when I would feel better and be over it. She laughed at me and said 'honey, we'll be talking about this for the next 15 years!' That was my last session. I learned three things from that therapist:

1. People have patterns. We do the same things over and over again.

2. He was abusive. There are forms of abuse that don't involve hitting. It turns out that threatening, yelling, and throwing knives counts even if they don't actually hit you.
3. I was NOT going to dedicate the next 15 years to getting over this schmuck.

I read everything I could about the abuse cycle and I learned it was a pattern. I deduced that if the pattern could be broken, everything would change. I was good friends with a kinesiologist chiropractor and a neurologist at the time. We figured there had to be a way to stop the pattern and to stop this from happening in the future.

That is when we sat around and decided to try this and that.

We knew the forehead would work because the neurosurgeon explained the electrochemical activity in the brain and where the centers of activity were. The chiropractor had a vast knowledge of eastern energy systems and noted that the chi corresponded to the same areas we were discussing. He knew ways to stimulate various areas of the brain's energy. Between the mapping the neurologist brought, the knowledge the chiropractor brought, and my experience, education, and intuition, the Lotus Seed Process (later renamed Lotus Seed Life) was born.

At first we tried a session to go give up caffeine. It worked. I didn't crave it and I didn't want it.

We then tried it on me and my cycle of abuse. I knew that if I could break one part of the cycle, it would be interrupted and things would work differently for me in the future. I would attract different men. I would be treated differently. I would feel differently about myself. The implications are endless.

I spent the next 20 years working with clients. We addressed whatever the most pressing issues were in their lives. I made up the sessions as I went. I knew what their trouble was, I knew what the positive opposite of the trouble was. Together, we would work through an issue in one session. Then we could sit back and watch the changes manifest. It was great fun.

I worked with hundreds of people and took thousands of pages of notes. Most were on napkins, receipts, and other scraps. I filed them for each client to keep a record of their work and progress.

I was helping people. I was helping lots of people deal with their patterns and problems. I helped people with addictions. I helped people through grief. I helped people with divorces and marriages. I helped people have kids taught them how to parent. I helped people with their jobs and careers. For a time I was paid big bucks to be a business consultant after I saved one man £38,000 in taxes with one phone call. I helped put people in touch with themselves.

I wanted to take this on the road. I wanted to make it bigger and reach more people. I knew that I only had so many hours in a day. People would call when something happened that they wanted help with. They would call all hours day or night. It got to be a real hassle for them to get through because I was always on the phone. Sometimes they had to call for several hours straight in order to reach me.

I had as many clients as I could handle and more were coming to me every month.

Since then, Nate and I have assembled a manual listing key words and topics for each session. I have tested each session on hundreds of people since 2008, refining and polishing along the way. The 11th edition of our Specialist Manual now lists 178 sessions. It is a guide through everything that can afflict a person. Each session is a guide. It is not a script. Each person has an individual story. Everyone has things that are important to them and each person has their own set of baggage to work through. Some sessions will be huge for one person and polish for another.

Each person that applies to become a Lotus Seed Life Specialist is a graduate of the process and each is moved to make Lotus Seed their life. Each specialist is driven by extremely high ideals after experiencing extremely profound firsthand results. People who work for us have each said "you have changed my life more profoundly than anything I thought possible. I want to help others as you have helped me."

Light at the End of the Tunnel

By telling the story about my journey with Lotus Seed Life (LSL) I am really telling the story about me, my husband David and our 2 daughters because we have all at one time or another called upon LSL to help us.

We were introduced to Vikki and what then was known as "the process" back in 2005. For David and I it was a terrible time; my mother had passed away in January 2004 followed by a dear friend in May that year, our business was going through a period of losing money at an alarming rate and every time we tried new strategies to save it, somehow they all went wrong and cost us even more money.

Both our daughters were at private school and we really didn't know if we could keep them there, in fact at times it looked as though we would have to sell our home and start afresh from almost nothing.

We had been doing very well until the beginning of 2004 and of course the better you do, the more you commit financially – gradually we started to trim back on many of our outgoings. Insurances, entertainment, the girls' activities, buying clothes and any sort of social activity that involved money, these were all stopped.
Still things didn't improve - the worry, the stress and the distress didn't go away and we were beginning to feel like hamsters in a hamster wheel, running like mad and getting nowhere. In addition, we were suffering a massive dose of "teenage daughter"

syndrome with one of our daughters which was worse than all the other things put together – it really felt as though our lives were falling apart.

David and I began working with Vikki – we were really desperate and could only rely on a faith that LSL would help us because we really didn't know for sure that it would.

The big difference that LSL made to us at that time was that it helped us to see what was really important, that is our family and our health. We were given some "homework" to do, some of it was quite bizarre – I remember bouncing on a bed for 5 minutes (!) and promising Vikki that I wouldn't hoover the house for a week! This might sound strange but these things injected a little fun into our gloomy lives and helped us to relax a bit, helping us to focus on our real priorities.

Gradually as we relaxed and became a little happier, we could see that if the worst was to happen – so what??

We still had to make some very challenging decisions (as we all do) in our lives but with the support of Vikki our decisions seemed to be getting better; sometimes things still went badly wrong (like when our employee disappeared with our car and then crashed it) but we seemed to be holding a hand that guided us through the darkness and magically brought us to the light. That was LSL.

LSL didn't make us money but it did make us rich. It didn't solve our problems but it put them into perspective for us. It didn't banish our challenging teenager but it helped us to deal with her and love her until she outgrew it. LSL helped us to cope in a way that we never would have done on our own.

We gradually crawled back into our lives; it took 6 – 7 years. We have never regained what we lost financially in that time but we do now have an acceptable security gained by making better decisions under the watchful eye of LSL. Crucially those 6 – 7 years were not wasted with anger and despair, they were instead a learning process, a series of lessons from which we learned many things about ourselves and about life and about what is really important.

On the way we had a huge amount of fun, too! Visits to Denver and most memorably digging a fire pit in the deepest Colorado countryside all through the night. The reason was a visit from an Indian holy woman, Amma, which Vikki was involved with. And watching the sunrise at a canyon in Moab, Utah among many other precious memories.

We all came through this awful time and I really believe that we would not have survived in quite the same way without the help of Vikki and LSL

The last time I saw Vikki there was one thing hanging over that really bothered me – a burden of my own making that I was carrying and had no hope of putting right as it involved my dearest mum.

Without going into details, Vikki worked with me, it didn't take long, maybe 5 minutes but from that day to this my burden is no more and I am forever grateful to her for that because she took away an invisible barrier between me and my dead mother. That is priceless.

But we are all grateful to Vikki and LSL and will be forever. We went through a dark time and although we have no constant contact now I know that if we ever need LSL it will be there – and if LSL ever need us we will be there, too.

Thank you Vikki,
Diane Hudson

My Self Worth

A long time ago, in the north of Wales, I was born. I was born to a very loving couple. My father and his family were very loud and larger-than-life and my mother's side was quieter and reserved. Shortly after I was born my sister was born and as we grew up, I secretly wanted to be more like my sister because boys and people gravitated towards her. I often found myself comparing myself to her and I never felt I was as good as she was.

I went off to Manchester not knowing what I wanted to do in my life. I took a food technology course. It wasn't what I wanted but I worked in several laboratories testing foods. My life up until that point felt like I was a square peg trying to fit into a round hole. I didn't feel like I belonged in my family. I didn't feel like I belonged with friends. I didn't feel I belonged in the jobs I was getting. I felt very out of place.

While I was there I met Paul. He was in the Royal Air Force and I thought he was my ticket out of there. He was going through a divorce when I met him. He was in a lot of debt due to that marriage and divorce and money was very tight for us. I was four months along when I found out I was pregnant. I went my very family-oriented doctor to talk about my options. I was in great turmoil not knowing what to do - should I give the baby up for adoption? Should I keep the baby? What should I do? I had question after question after question. The doctor suggested that I keep the baby and as I was leaving the doctors office I remember thinking *I have no idea what I'm doing I am way out of my element.* I was scared. I was nervous.

Then I had to tell my parents. When I did my father blew up. My father's first words were "well I guess you better get married." So we did. We were married six months after I became pregnant. Paul and I moved to Scotland where Paul was stationed.

Four months later our daughter, Suzanne, was born. The pregnancy was very easy but the birth was very difficult. I was so afraid of being a new mom. I was afraid not knowing how to take care of the baby. I was afraid of not wanting the baby. I was afraid of Paul leaving me. I was afraid of all the responsibility and being too young to handle it all. All of that fear made it a difficult birth. The baby had to be taken out with forceps it was very painful.

After the birth I lost a lot of weight and became very anemic. My milk dried up and I didn't know what to do. I called the midwife in and she gave me infant formula. Eventually both the baby and I started to gain weight. We both became more healthy. In the meantime, Paul didn't want my family there to help me so I was on my own for most of it. After about a year, I decided that Suzanne needed a sibling so we tried for another baby. I had a miscarriage.

At this time Paul decided he had had enough of the RAF so, without consulting me, he bought himself out and decided he was moving back to Yorkshire. Paul started a multilevel marketing business which was draining our finances. Then Paul bought a fancy car in order to impress potential clients. The business ate up all of our money to the point that we didn't have food. We kept trying for another baby. After about two years I became pregnant with Abby. That was when Paul came to me and told me I should go back to North Wales and live with my parents because there was not enough money. His plan was for me to live with my parents and for him to live with his mom, get a job, and save money. Then we would all live together.

Eventually we got back together and we were together for two years. But Paul had lived the single life for far too long and didn't want to take care of a wife and two children. He decided he didn't want to be married anymore. I did what most women do and said "you can't leave because of the children!" At that time, Paul could only think about himself and his needs and his happiness and he left us. In hindsight, the truth of the matter was his leaving was the best thing he did. But at the time, it was a very difficult for me to be a single mom with two children.

He moved and started working in France. He was in his 30's and dating 18-year-olds who wanted nothing to do with my girls. His lifestyle was about partying with his mates and different girlfriends. He didn't have the time or the desire to be a father. I believe that he was unfaithful, even though at the time, I didn't want to see it. I didn't want to believe it but looking back on it all the signs were there.

As the girls grew up Paul saw them very sporadically when and if he felt like it. Suzanne was devastated. She was daddy's little girl and wanted daddy to love her like she loved him. It was never going to happen. He never really wanted them. As I look back on it now, I think Suzanne blamed me for her daddy leaving and all of her penned up hurt and pain came out at me as anger and rage because I was the one around.

As Suzanne turned 13 she decided that she didn't want to go see her dad anymore. Paul never treated them as family as he was too busy partying and being with his latest girlfriends to pay any attention to his daughters. Suzanne and Abby both felt very unwanted and more of a burden to their dad. They were both very uncomfortable at his house. This is the time that Suzanne decided that she was done with her dad.

Abby wanted to continue to see him. Then, when she turned about 12 she wrote her dad a letter telling him exactly how she felt. She told him that she wanted to try to have a relationship with him. She explained that she felt hurt and uncomfortable around him. Paul never bothered to acknowledge the letter or do anything to facilitate a relationship with either one of the girls. That was the last time he saw her.

The girls were great and we had our ups and downs as mothers and daughters do. They both enjoyed school. They both were happy and fun-loving girls. I was doing the best I knew how. I admittedly didn't know how to parent. I thought the only way to parent was like my parents had; with a loving but stern hand.

As Suzanne got into puberty she became more and more stubborn and willful. I didn't know how to make her do what I wanted. The more power I exerted the more rebellious she became. The further into the teenage years, the more Suzanne challenged me. She challenged my authority. The more stubborn she became the more angry I became. When she got more angry the anger would erupt into rage. We would have terrible fights. Some of these fights were not only shouting and yelling at each other but would develop into physically throwing things. I remember on several different occasions the dinner plates would go flying against the wall. After everyone had gone to bed and I was cleaning it up I would cry to myself. It was being proved to me that I didn't know what to do or how to parent. I blamed myself and felt terribly guilty.

At different times I wanted Suzanne to feel as terrible as she made me feel. I often felt like a terrible mother. I didn't know how to change things. I was very unhappy. I spent a lot of time crying and racking my brain to see what I could do to make things better. My self-worth had gone into the toilet. I didn't believe in myself. I couldn't make a decision for myself. I didn't deserve anything good because I was so bad. I was a mean and horrible mother. There were so many negative thoughts going through my mind that I couldn't do anything right. I was very unhappy. Suzanne was also very unhappy. Our relationship was shattered.

I needed to do something so I started training in different holistic practices, spiritual healing, cranial sacral therapy, Reiki, and aromatherapy. Every time I tried something new I thought that possibly *this* was going to be what changed my pattern with Suzanne. Each thing I tried worked for a little while but all the negative thoughts came flooding back in. I truly wanted a relationship with Suzanne. I didn't know how to change my pattern. The power struggle between us would creep in and cause another fight and another explosion.

One of the courses that I took was called "__ ____ Massage" and as I started my qualifications as a master practitioner, the business owner would give us these rigorous exams which I failed time after time. Failing these exams added to my lack of confidence. During this time I met another person that was trying to qualify for his mastery in massage. We found out that the teacher and qualifier kept changing the passing criteria on us. He was sabotaging us so that we would take the course again which meant more money for him. I believed what the qualifier told me when he told me that I was no good at massage. I would take the course again and fail the exam again.

Now my mindset was that of a true failure. I couldn't qualify as a massage therapist. I had a terrible relationship, if you could even call it a relationship, with my oldest daughter. My love life was nonexistent. I was barely scraping by financially. Nothing in my life was working.

The man that I met in the massage course was Julian. He was a lovely guy. He was a breath of fresh air. Julian was the one who introduced me to Lotus Seed Life (LSL). He talked about how LSL had changed his life. He talked about all the self-help courses and weekends and retreats that he had been on it had not worked. He was excited and empowered about all the patterns that LSL had changed in his life. His enthusiasm and vivacious nature was infectious. Talking to him gave me hope. It opened the door for me to possibly have a relationship with Suzanne. However, like many people, I didn't take his advice. I sat on the phone number for 4 to 6 months.

During this time Suzanne and I fought even more. The fights continued to be very explosive and hurtful to both of us. As things got progressively worse in those 4 to 6 months I found myself at the emergency room with a gash in my head knowing that I couldn't do this anymore. I had nothing to lose so why not give LSL a call?

I went home from the emergency room to call the number that Julian had given me. We had our first session and I didn't feel very much. As I did more sessions I started to feel relaxed. I started to feel like something in me was changing but I didn't know what. I started to feel lighter and more positive. I decided to sign up for the entire course.

I use to take everything that Suzanne did and said very personally. I would always talk back to her and be very quick with my tongue and sometimes mean. I could feel very incensed. When Suzanne would scream and shout and was rude to me it would tap into all of my insecurities and everything that I was doing wrong. It would also tap into all of my inadequacies and worries. When she tapped into everything I would shout back and the fights would escalate.

I remember this one particular time after doing several sessions that she came in shouting and being very rude. I just stood there, I didn't answer back. I did nothing. This was very unusual for me and I learned that if I didn't answer back then it doesn't fuel the fight in the argument! It doesn't escalate things. I kept my mouth shut and just listened to her for the very first time. I empathized with her. When she was finished yelling and ranting and raving she just walked off. I didn't feel bad for yelling at her I didn't take anything personally. I just let her be. All she wanted was to be heard! That was the time, in that very moment, that I knew LSL was making a change in my life. My pattern was changing.

It was then that I started to take a look at my life. I noticed that my pattern with Suzanne was changing. My business patterns were changing because I valued myself at a deep core level and therefore I was able to charge what I was worth in my business.

I always tried to control everything; my parents, my studies, my husband, my kids, my business, my money, and my dancing. My dance partners would often say to me "You are leading, let me lead." After noticing a pattern with Suzanne, I noticed that I was letting my dance partner lead. When I finally stopped trying to control everyone and everything, everything became a lot easier. When I let my dance partner lead I became more fluid and more into the music and was able to bring my creativity and a lot of feeling and passion to the dance.

I believe that LSL changed my life, Suzanne's life, and Abbi's life.

After completing be entireLSL course, I was such a different person that I wanted to help others to achieve their goals like I was able to achieve mine. I trained to be a LSL specialist. I have loved every minute working with clients and watching them experience a different mindset in their lives. It often overwhelms me and brings tears to my eyes when I see my clients becoming the beautiful loving empowered people that they are.

I have a lot of admiration respect and reverence for the LSL founder, Vikki Faudel. I do not know where I would be if I had not made that initial phone call. I hope that reading my story it will resonate with people so much that they will want to make the changes in their lives.

Thank you for being in my life and changing my life. Thank you for teaching, supporting, and unconditionally loving me.

I can hardly wait to see where the next chapter of my story takes me!

Gill Wright

The World is My Oyster

"The thing that is really hard, and really amazing, is giving up on being perfect and beginning the work of becoming yourself."

Anna Quindlen

As an individual I have always thought I have been doing well in life. I had a good job as an engineer. I had the opportunity to live and explore many places around the UK. I played number of sports. I had a good social life. I was lucky to find a kind and loving husband. But underlying all this, I have never truly felt fulfilled or that I had reached my full potential.

Then about two years ago (2015), I was diagnosed by the doctors with post-viral syndrome. Essentially I felt awful all the time and I didn't want to do anything. I found excuses to avoid seeing friends. Anytime I did exercise I would feel exhausted for days afterwards. I started to miss days at work. My relationship started to have difficulties. I felt there was no way out. I never thought this would happen to me. I always thought people who complained about these types of illnesses were just not trying hard enough. I can safely say now that that was a very naïve attitude. I saw a number of doctors at the time. Although they were very supportive they didn't have a fix-all solution. I started reading up on my condition but again there was no conclusive evidence as to why this happens or how to fix it. I then started trying alternative methods such as acupuncture and alternative medicines but again it never seemed to make much difference.

Then 18 months ago, someone suggested I try Lotus Seed Life (LSL). The person I spoke with had been working with LSL and they had started seeing improvements in their life. I was quite skeptical at first but after speaking to Vikki (creator of LSL) and reading the LSL website I decided to give it a go. Gill Wright was suggested to me as a good specialist match and I started my first session.

Within a month, if not sooner, I started to make huge improvements. Don't get me wrong, it was not an overnight cure. But I started to feel like I could go out and do things; small things to start like visiting places and going out for walks. Within three months I started to show significant improvements at work. Even my bosses were starting to notice and remarked on my improved attitude and work output. I was also starting to notice improved confidence.

It is all a bit of a blur from there but my life seems to be going from strength to strength. I got promoted at work earlier this year and am now seen as "one to watch." My relationship is better than ever. I took on the Couch to 5K challenge and am now regularly running 5K. I had never run before in my life! I have started weight training in a small gym which had never occurred to me before. I really enjoy it. LSL is making a big difference to my confidence.

That is just the start, I can go on and on!

All of this has been great but I think my biggest change for me is that I'm starting to explore things I really enjoy in life. And believing "The World is my Oyster" I feel I still have a way to go with further improvements but I now know I can continue to grow and develop opportunities in my life. I'm looking forward to continuing with LSL to see what happens next.

Thank you so much to Gill and LSL. You have helped me to turn my life around and upside down. I now know how important "looking after me" is and what a difference it makes to my life.

Kate,

Berkshire UK

My Own Voice

It's slightly strange to look back over the past while and see (in my mind's eye) the man I used to be compared to the man I am today. There has been a huge amount of change.

When I started having sessions with Lotus Seed Life (LSL), I had major issues and problems dealing with conflict and with binge eating - I'd struggled with my weight for over 30 years.

Now I find myself in a place where the desire to buy and consume large amounts of junk food (to bury uncomfortable feelings I didn't know how to deal with) for a binge has pretty much gone. I honestly wondered if that day would ever come. Not only did I binge and consume large amounts of food I also consumed large amounts of media (films & TV). Well, I wasn't binge eating all the time, but I was quite often sat in front of the TV at home or at the cinema. Now, there's nothing wrong with doing some viewing from time to time, the problem comes, as with anything, when it's taken to extremes.

I've done a lot of personal growth & development over the years having read literally hundreds of personal development books, listened to many many hours of personal development audio, been to many seminars and events and trained in Neuro-Linguistic Programming (NLP) to master practitioner level. I've also had some coaching and therapy in various guises and I can say, with my hand on my heart, while all those things helped to a degree, they all pale in comparison to the changes and massive shifts I've been able to make in myself with LSL. It's a like being in a model T Ford driving along at about 40 miles per hour and then changing over to a formula one racing car (far more efficient vehicle) which enables you to fly down the road in excess of 200mph.

Over the years I have suffered at the hands of many bullies and abusive people (including an abusive mother) and cowered in fear, sometimes literally physically. More often, in adult life, on the inside mentally and emotionally. When confronted with a situation where someone was being unpleasant or rude or abusive toward me and there was conflict, I'd get incredibly nervous; my guts would churn like a washing machine and my mind would go blank. This meant I couldn't think straight to be able to see through what they were doing. I couldn't fully hear and understand the nonsense and outright bullying behaviour that someone was attempting to perpetrate on me.

I was not able to respond appropriately. As a result I would often be taken advantage of. I would end up in a situation where I was repeatedly trying to refuse to do what they wanted me to or trying to refuse to buy their product. My responses were ineffective. At first they wouldn't take no for an answer or it would go on for ages until they eventually gave up. I knew the high likelihood that the situation would recur in the near future. This was far from ideal.

These days things are incredibly different. When it comes to conflict or someone trying to take advantage of me, or attempting to abuse me, (I say trying and attempting because they don't get away with it anymore) I can handle it.

In the last year I've had to deal with a few people who have been difficult, rude and unreasonable and I've handled it incredibly differently to how I used to. I informed one person, in no uncertain terms, that their behaviour was unacceptable. Rather than my reaction being at the extreme of aggressive, or the other extreme of passive like I used to be, it was in that wonderfully confident middle ground of assertion where I called attention to, and focused on, their behaviour and how it was unacceptable. Sometimes it's surprising how effective something really simple can be.

I am now at a point in my life where I am no longer a doormat and no one abuses or tries to bully me. This all relates to how and what I feel and think about myself. This comes out in everything I say and do; how I conduct myself and how I live my life.

Growth can be subtle. There are times where I didn't notice the effects of the sessions until something happened to show me I had grown. I experienced that in relation to someone in my life who had repeatedly used emotional blackmail and manipulation to get their way with me. It was only after an angry seven minute phone call from this person that I realized just how far I'd come in this regard. During this call they tried their usual stuff; getting progressively more and more angry. I responded calmly, listened to what was said each time, and pointed out the lack of logic in it. Thus reinforced the good, sensible, and well-meaning reasons I had done the thing they were mad about in the first place. Previously, I would have crumpled like a soft drink can but this time they did not get away with it. I was glad it was over but unlike previous calls, I wasn't wiped out emotionally and mentally, or paralyzed by nerves. To date this person hasn't attempted to behave like that toward me again and most likely never will.

So what about the eating stuff? Well, like I said earlier, it's so much better than it was. Cooking was something I never used to do, at least proper cooking from scratch with healthy ingredients. Anyone can nuke a ready meal. The other day I cooked my fiance a meal from scratch with healthy ingredients which she really appreciated and told me she felt loved as a result.

I'm still overweight but I'm relaxed about it. I love who I am and how I look. I know that gradually, sensibly, over a reasonable period of time, I will reduce and release weight to get down to my ideal healthy weight which I will then be able to maintain with ease.

I'd only been having LSL sessions for a few months when I was admitted to hospital with two infections that were very serious. I spent a week in the intensive care ward until being moved to different wards for another two weeks. Those three weeks were one of, if not the most difficult and trying times I've ever had in my life. When I was finally discharged and could come home I said to my fiance that I think I'd cried more during those three weeks than at any time in my adult life.

Without having the support of Vicki Wright and the LSL team, it would have been even more difficult. It was such an incredible relief to be able to call and talk things through both while I was in hospital and when I was home. I must have spent the first half of the session after I got home venting my frustrations about things before we got onto doing some statements. They expected that and allowed for it.

I did have a mini session while in hospital which helped me massively to better cope with it all.
It took me a few months to recover and heal until I was well enough to go back to work. In fact, the first quarter of that year was spent convalescing; not how I would have liked to start that year.

That year was rough for other reasons. Following my illness and healing, my fiance's mum died. In November, her father passed away, too. She had a lot of grief to deal with and it was hard to see her so upset but I'd learned from LSL that the healthy way to deal with grief is not to suppress it. Grief needs to be expressed and released. One day, Vikki advised us to watch a sad movie to help get in touch with our feelings around our loss. We did and after the movie ended she went up to the bedroom and absolutely sobbed her heart out. It was incredibly hard for me to stay downstairs and hear her like this but I knew I had to leave her to express it. Crying was what she needed. If I'd gone and comforted her it would have impeded her being able to fully experience all the grief. I was there for her in the next room but it wasn't easy. She knew I was there for her but we both knew she needed some time by herself.

What you learn from the wisdom of the LSL coaches is priceless, and incredibly useful in life, and you also develop the ability to be able to better handle tough situations.

I'm much more relaxed generally, but also in my relationship. I'm not trying too hard like I was in the early days.

A little while back I took on a role, in a voluntary capacity, for something that needed to be changed. To achieve what I thought was needed, I took a lot of work alongside my regular job. It was sometimes stressful and it meant dealing with some difficulties and unreasonable people. While it was much easier for me than it would have been had I not been working with LSL, there were still some challenging times that brought more lessons up for me to work on. As usual, Vicki had the exact right session at the right time and I kept on growing and releasing the emotional baggage I needed to. I did put a lot of mental time and energy into this role and got a bit obsessed for a while. It all worked out OK in the end. I achieved what I needed to and learned and grew plenty in the process.

Here's something I'd invite you to consider: when tough times or something comes up in your life don't say "Here we go again" instead say "Here we grow again." Every challenge or difficulty in our lives is an opportunity to learn something or grow; sometimes both. There's no better place or way to do so than by working with the LSL team.

Thank you,

Ray Stantz

Work is Play

I had my first Lotus Seed Life (LSL) session way back in 2011. At the time I was two years into a business venture with two other partners and was failing. It was only going downhill with no reprieve in sight. It affected my mood, my attitude towards others, as well as friendships and relationships. I had no confidence and I had turned into a complete recluse. I also couldn't deal with any additional setbacks or issues that came my way.

I started LSL with Geoff Sober, who was actually a client of mine at my gym at the time, based on the recommendations of my business partners who both had tried sessions. I was skeptical but Geoff convinced me by simply showcasing his skills. I asked a few questions about it and he pinpointed in a sentence what was going on in my life without me even telling him anything. This wasn't one of those general statements that applies to everyone, this was dead on and specific.

So two years of weekly LSL sessions ensued and I am eternally grateful for their help. I say "their" as Geoff helped me initially but Vikki has been able to take on the challenge more recently as different lessons have landed in my lap. Vikki won't mind me saying that I didn't like the first phone call with her! Sometimes the truth is hard to hear and change isn't easy but persevering through it has been more than worth it.

So, five years later, here are the results. Business has changed drastically. I own and strategically run 2 businesses that both encompass my life goals. In fact, business is so good I consider myself semi-retired and work is play. I am now engaged and getting married in under 6 weeks to the love of my life. (The date was March 31st 2017.) I am happy. I am confident. I have the tools to be able to deal with problems or what might be considered setbacks in a calm and efficient manner.

LSL is such a huge part of my life that I am now a practitioner, my mum is training to be one, and my staff will all be completing it this year, too! I am even blessed enough to have both Vikki & Geoff attend my wedding.

Tom Hibbert

Freedom!

I am the eldest of 4 siblings. We had a strict upbringing by both our parents. By strict I mean we had rules to adhere to such as having to go to bed at a set time and to go to church. My clothes were bought at a particular shop where my mom had an account. It was not a cheap shop so we got the clothes that my mom picked out for us. I recall that I wanted a pair of jeans to be just like the other kids but my father did not like females in jeans so it never happened. My parents regimen was based on the 50's mentality. The times everywhere else were progressing into the 60's and 70's but my parents did not change. As children we knew not to rock the boat at home.

I left school at 17 and went to an affluent secretarial school in London. I met a lot of different girls, most of whom were debutantes from very wealthy families. I qualified for and began working in the fashion industry which was wonderful. I loved my job. It was sometimes hectic and very long hours but it was great for me.

At age 25 I met my husband, Nick, through a flatmate. He had a good job and I was working. We were making sufficient money. One day after we got engaged; he got angry and out of the blue. He hit me. I forgave him.

I married him at age 26. We moved into his flat in the countryside. He didn't want to move into my flat in London. We did what he wanted. I had to start a new life in a new location. I was isolated. Then a few months later he got angry and hit me again. I forgave him again and again <u>for the next 25 years.</u> He drank. He would go out with workmates and clients and not come home until 2 or 3 or 4 in the morning. He would tell me he was entertaining clients. I believed him for a while. Then I realized that he wasn't with clients that he was just going out drinking with friends, colleagues and sometimes other women. I could not bring myself to tell my parents what a mess I had made of my life. All I wanted to do was flee. But I couldn't; I didn't have the strength.

There were often times I would have dinner waiting for him and he wouldn't come home. I got pregnant with my first child at 27. My first child was a beautiful daughter named Rachael. Then, 18 months later I had my son named Tom. (Tom's story was just previous to mine.) We'd moved house again. I had to start my life over again in another new location. This time I got involved in a mother/children group. The other ladies there became my friends and we're still friends today. I never talked about Nick hitting me or the emotional abuse. But I know there were telltale signs, like wearing a scarf on a hot day and wearing long sleeves in the summer. I'm sure these friends were afraid to talk to me about it as well. But they knew. When my oldest son, Tom, was 4 years old, Nick had an affair. Yes you guessed it, I forgave him again. I then had another baby, Charlie. A few years went by. When Charlie was 4, Nick had another affair. I dug my heels in and wanted him to leave. I told him to leave but he wouldn't go. So I forgave him...again. We moved house and the abuse carried on. My husband wasn't hitting me every week but he was very cleverly controlling. He had the life he wanted and I had to fit in with him together with the three kids.

He was, and is, a master manipulator. He controlled everything. He controlled who I talked to. He controlled what I did. He controlled our money. He had plenty of money to drink. I had to make do with what was left over to buy food and clothing for the kids. I had to pretend that everything was okay.

I started studying French and needlework. When I wasn't in my daily duties I studied. This is how I coped with everything. I didn't have any time to think about the abuse.

My husband got a transfer to New Jersey, USA. I had to set up a new life for myself and my children who were 14, 13, and 9 years old. He worked in New York. While he was working in New York he was involved in 9/11. The building where he was working was damaged by one of the planes. He was traumatized. He was offered treatment and counseling but he refused it. The 9/11 incident made his abuse worse. After 9/11 he took early retirement and we moved back to the UK for 18 months. Rachael was at College and Tom and Charlie were at school. We moved again to France. Tom went to University. Nick wanted our youngest child, Charlie, to go to an international school in France but he didn't want us to live near the school. I had one child at home and cared for my elderly mother-in-law. I knew I didn't have any choices in anything. My voice was never heard, my opinion had no value. The control continued with every move. His yelling and shouting was getting worse and more frequent. I didn't see any options for me to get out of the relationship.

I remember one of the incidents was on a summer day in France when I had all the children home and my niece and nephew were there was well. Nick was drinking wine in order to cool down. By evening he was pretty well drunk. After clearing up dinner, the girls were excited to be going out to a Country and Western evening in a neighbouring village. The boys got out a board game when, all of a sudden, Nick lost it. He started shouting and yelling and throwing things. Tom ran out of the house and into the surrounding fields. Shouting continued for a while. Then Nick took the keys and locked the house so no one could enter or leave. He slept with the keys under his pillow. I managed to calm my niece and nephew down. I quietly snuck upstairs and packed a bag for everyone. I snuck the keys. In the morning all six of us squeezed into a small car. I dropped three of them off at the airport so they could fly back to England. The other three of us started our journey back to the UK by car. Nick had canceled all my credit cards and I just had enough fuel to make the 800-mile journey thanks to my daughter's job.

Over the years he would verbally abuse the children. I always managed to get between my children and my husband to deflate the situation. I remember being in France waiting for Charlie's last exam results. The last exam was in math which was his weakest subject. We were all a little on edge. I had left the room and when I returned I found my husband had had Charlie up against the wall aggressively with his arm pressed against Charlie's throat. All because he did not believe that Charlie had passed math. I sent Charlie back to London immediately.

I returned to France after four months and started legal divorce proceedings. I started a computer course which led me to apply at the University. After six weeks at the University I was diagnosed with rectal cancer so I took a year off from school. During this time, my mother passed away. After completion of my course at the University I returned back to my father's house. He passed away shortly after my return.

I was still dealing with the marriage breakdown, the abuse, both parents passing away and my own cancer. So many emotions and situations to deal with. . .

My first year at the University my son, Tom, saw that I needed help as I felt that I was struggling and I could not study. I was crying a lot. He said that he could not help me but he knew someone who could. Tom put me in contact with Geoff Sober, a Lotus Seed Life (LSL) specialist. I started LSL sessions with

Geoff. My sessions were not regular but were linked to dates that I had to complete a university assignment. The sessions helped me accept that I was worthy to be at the University. I was to say the least, a bit depressed and crying, and this was unlike me. Thanks to my strict upbringing I normally kept my emotions in control. Because of my abusive marriage my feelings had been in check since the age of 26. I had learned to be an unfeeling adult, emotional yet in control. I had not dealt with any of the emotions that I had felt over the past many years. I had not dealt with the victimization in the marriage, the anger, the helplessness, and the feeling that I was utterly worthless. I didn't even know what the emotions were that I was feeling. I just knew that all I wanted to do was cry.

LSL helped me get through my assignments at the University. I didn't feel a great deal of change until I started doing regular sessions weekly and sometimes twice-weekly. From the very beginning, it helped me feel calm and I had a clarity in my thinking so I was able to focus on my University work. LSL made it possible for me to find a path in life. I was able to take on the teaching course where I taught English to foreign adults. LSL gave me my worth back and the confidence to meet other groups of people. Friends of mine would say I had a glow about me and that I didn't seem so depressed. I started wearing brighter clothes. LSL helped me to be able to call my friends again. Some of these examples seem like little things but they made a world of difference in my life. They all added up to giving back my confidence. I found my purpose. I know my life matters. I know I can make a difference to others.

I don't dwell on the negative. I have learned through LSL to deal with it and move on.

My youngest son Charlie lives with me, Tom lives a quarter of an hour away, Rachael lives in France and we talk constantly. I am dealing with some health issues at the present moment. The one thing about LSL is that it helps me cope with all of the different treatments and to stay positive during this journey. Recently I was in the hospital and I was able to speak with Vikki regarding how I was feeling. She listened. We did a session and once again I could deal with everything.

Unfortunately, my cancer has returned but I know that with my family, friends, and the LSL team, the time I have remaining will be glorious. As they say in America, "I will go out with a bang" thanks to Vikki.

I am very grateful for the support that I have received from my family. I'm extremely grateful to Tom for introducing me to LSL. I feel luckier than most because I know that, with my support system, I will have the quality of life I deserve and I want.

My advice to anyone would be: if you can see a parallel between my story and yours to pick up the phone and speak to someone in the LSL team. Do it now. After doing sessions both sporadically, and on a weekly basis, I recommend you have regular sessions. They are more beneficial. I know you don't realize how beneficial until after you see and feel the changes in your life.

Thank you,
Angela

My Own Choices

In my 20's I didn't have very many relationships. The relationships all started out with lots of potential. I was optimistic. I was hopeful of something long-term. But sadly, all my relationship ended between two and four months. A lot of the relationships ended because we wanted different things. I wanted a partner who was going to go places with me; a partner who would appreciate me for who I was, someone who would be loyal to me and our relationship. I wanted a partner who would be as attentive to me as I was to him. I wanted to be treated with respect. I wanted to be treated like I mattered. I wanted to be treated like I was the most important thing in his life. I wanted a true partner to share everything with. I wanted it to last. I was attracting and choosing men who just wanted fun for a few weeks. Instead, they were men who wanted what they could get from me and then they were gone. The men I was attracting were also, let's say, not nice. For example, one guy I dated was so jealous of me and of my friends he would often shout at me. When we went anywhere together I had to be right next to him. If we were at a friend's house I couldn't even be in a different room. His jealousy would manifest by accusing me of being unfaithful.

Between my relationships there were long periods of being on my own. At this time I suffered from frustration and loneliness. I was on the verge of a depression. I didn't really see any progress happening at work. I was living in a new area and didn't know anybody socially. A lot of the people I knew from work and from my past were getting into long-term relationships and even getting married. This added to my frustration and I started to question myself about what was wrong with me. Why couldn't I be in a relationship? Why couldn't I be happy? Why wasn't I good enough? I asked "why" a lot. I felt as though everything was my fault. I didn't fit in. I really didn't like anything about my life.

One of my colleagues invited me to a salsa dance class. My girlfriend and I had some really good times at those classes. At one particular class I met a man named Rob. We danced a few dances and chatted a bit. After few weeks of chatting at dance class we began dating. He treated me well. He was very nice to me. He seemed committed to the relationship. He treated me like I was special. It seemed that we both wanted the same kinds of things in life. There were a lot of signs that seem to tell me that the relationship was going somewhere. A month later for Christmas he bought me lots of presents and introduced me to his mom which gave me lots of hope for the future. Unfortunately it was false hope because right after New Year's he told me he didn't want to be in a relationship. We carried on seeing each other and doing things together. In my mind I wanted to be in a relationship so bad that I put up with whatever he said. Even though he didn't want to be in a relationship, I believed we were.

Everything started to be on his terms. He was very attentive as long as was his idea. If it was my idea he he would reject me in a mean manner. It was almost like he was saying "how dare I ask to go and do something fun with me? My time is more important than whatever it was you were suggesting." Looking back on it, I would say he was narcissistic. He gave me a lot of mixed messages through the entire relationship. I made a lot of excuses for his actions and his words. I said things like "he's overworked," "His work is stressful." and "I'm asking for too much."

It lasted a total of 2 ½ months. In February he went on holiday by himself. He came back and told me he had met someone else on holiday and he was done with me. It was the day before Valentine's Day. I had a real hard time with it being over because he was so kind, generous and caring. Looking back on it, the pattern was that he was nice for a while, then he was mean for couple days and then he was back to being his nice loving self. Even though he said it was over he kept calling me. He kept coming by to see me and drew me back in. This was the time that he introduced me to the Lotus Seed Life (LSL). He told me that we couldn't be in a long-term relationship, because I am not very good at relationships. He also told me that I was giving him mixed messages and I didn't know what I wanted.

I trusted him, he seemed like a guy who had his life together, so when he said I should give LSL a try I decided to do just that. I worked with Vikki Faudel. In the beginning I was very skeptical. The first time I talked to Vikki she actually listened to me. She listened in such a way that I knew she cared. She didn't just hear my words, she listened with her whole heart.

I started meeting and dating other guys. While this was going on Rob was doing all he could to make sure that I didn't have a steady relationship. I felt as though he wanted to make sure that I was there when his relationship ended. He would show up and say nasty things to my dates. We would be at parties together with other people and he would say things to me and them to cause doubt.

After doing a few sessions I became the strong one. This is when I decided that it was over and I wanted nothing more to do with him. It was quite hard but I had to tell him I didn't want him around. I came to the conclusion that he was not good for me. He was using me and keeping me around in case it didn't work with the other woman. For a while I let him. Then I was the one that said it's totally over. I was done. I wasn't going to allow him to treat me that way anymore. This is all down to LSL.

I noticed that after doing sessions things just seem to flow a lot easier. Driving was easier. I seemed to get more green lights. Everything was just in the flow. I started to feel like I had genuine confidence, not pretend confidence that some of us put on. I had been doing sessions now for about four or five months and was seeing some real changes.

Then, one day Vikki and I did a session on saying "NO" too much. My homework after the session was to say "yes" to 3 things that I would normally say "no" to. Shortly after that session ended there was a knock on the door. The local karate studio was having a student drive. They were trying to get new students to enroll. So I said "yes." That was the biggest change of my entire life....

I followed through and went to the karate club. In the karate club I can be myself. No one had any preconceived ideas of me. I had a clean slate just to be myself with no pretense.

I was in karate for 5 months before I went to my first grading and received my yellow belt. That excitement of accomplishing something on my own caused me to really commit to karate. I continued to progress. I started competing in different tournaments. Nine years from the time I first started I hold several different titles. I have also won several different medals. I am a world karate champion. As of 2017, I have earned Nidan, which is a high rank in the karate world. A lot of these divisions I was competing against ladies who were considerably younger than me. At these tournaments I often did LSL statements on myself prior to each comp which put me in a winning mindset against ladies who were considerably younger than me.

I decided to join a dating website where I met a lot of nice people and went on some dates. If it hadn't been for LSL I would not have had the nerve to join a dating website. I could allow myself to have fun with it. I could now tell people how I felt and not worry about their reactions. I could be honest with them and not give them the false hope.

I met a man, his name was Mark. Mark and I had a lot of synchronicity between us. The relationship was really easy and we had some shared interests. We lasted 2 ½ years because we were comfortable. During the course of the relationship, Mark suffered from anxiety and didn't want to go out to do things which was okay with me because I was happy staying at home as well.

The problem was when we went on holiday and had plans. We would have paid for it but at the last minute he would say he wasn't going.

I remember being on holiday in America. We would have things planned and he would just say "No, I don't want to do it." The first couple of times we didn't do something he didn't want to. Sometimes it would take a lot of coaxing to get him out of the hotel room. Then I got angry and said I would go do things without him. I did and I had a blast. He even ordered take out to the hotel to avoid leaving the room.

His anxiety was getting worse and worse. We weren't even able to go out for a meal. If I made him go or do something he didn't want to do, like go to one of my karate competitions, he would throw a temper tantrum. These temper tantrums would last for days. He would scream and shout and cuss at me. He wasn't dealing with any of his anxiety issues. Being in a relationship was too much pressure for him to handle. He liked having the anxiety because it gave him control over others as everyone tried to help him. He didn't really want the help as much as the attention. He would not even consider working with Lotus Seed Life, or any other therapies. All he could think about was himself. He ended it with me because he said I was too adventurous.

Let's talk about career. Big changes happened for me there due to LSL. I am an educator in the school system. I have been in the system for many years. The more I've been in the system, the more I've learned I don't want to be in the system. I wanted to help the students but I couldn't because of the rules and regulations. Because of all the constraints of the system I decided that I wanted to be a Lotus Seed Life specialist. I remember thinking that if I could get paid to leave the education system that I would start my Lotus Seed Life training. Eventually the school where I worked was offering voluntary paid redundancy. I took it. I started my training as a Lotus Seed Life specialist. Now I am a certified LSL specialist. I have clients of my own. I am happy that I get to help people like I was helped.

Back to my relationships. My female karate sensei strongly suggested that there might be someone right underneath my nose that was very interested in me. She suggested I give him some consideration. Over the next few weeks I started chatting with him. I was a little reserved because I was just out of a relationship. I knew that if this relationship didn't work out it might be very awkward because we were both in the same karate club. I found I really liked him but I didn't want to admit it. We went out on a proper date early in early in the year. Things started to blossom. There are major differences between this relationship and my past relationships. The best part is that I like him for who he is and he likes me for who I am. We're not in this relationship to change the other person. We are secure in who we are both as individuals and in the partnership. He is there to support me during my championships in karate or even if I just had a bad day. I can rely on him. I know he will be there if I'm sick or hurt. He genuinely cares about my well-being. It's also a comforting thought to know that he knows that I have been and will be there for him. He also appreciates me for what I do for him and his kids. He feels the love that LS L has taught me to show and express.

I was lucky enough to go on a LSL retreat in Colorado in

2016. This was 10 days with Vikki and her husband, Nate. This was my most memorable and exciting part of LSL as of today. The people on the retreat were clients of mine, clients of other specialists, specialists, and specialists in training. This was a place where everyone came together as a community. We did things together; the cooking, the dishes, yoga, everything. We did a lot of fun things. We went to a water park. We hiked in the Rocky Mountains. We crossed a large suspension bridge and saw gorgeous views. I felt like I was on top of the world. We went to a ghost town. We stayed in this wonderful, beautiful, cool mountain cabin. We went white water rafting. Partway down the river we had the opportunity to get out of the boat to climb up onto a big rock and jump into the water. I have a lot of respect for gravity so the thought of doing this was a little nerve-racking but I knew I had to do it. I got out of the water, I climbed up on the rock, I closed my eyes and I jumped. I opened my eyes just as my feet were leaving the rock. I did it! I learned so much about myself and others by jumping off a rock. The whole experience was so much fun and exciting.

One night on the retreat I got an empty fortune cookie. I was sad for a second because I thought it meant I didn't have a fortune. Vikki said to me, what it means is "you get to make your own fortune." Before LSL, I would've been scared on my wits with that thought but now I find it exciting. There are so many possibilities.

Before LSL I was frustrated with not being good enough for other people. Wanting to be different also trying to figure out how I could be different so I could be good enough. Now I know I can do anything because for the first time in my life I believe in me. I know I am good enough. I know I'm the best me I can be. If I try something and I don't get it I know I can do it again and that's okay. With every small failure I am closer to a huge success.

For the first time in my life I can say I am truly happy. It's hard to think about myself and think about the way I was so long ago. I'm so glad to not be that way anymore. Now I am calmer and more confident. Now when there's bumps in the road, which we know there always will be, I know I can handle it. I'm so happy to be me; the genuine me, not the me that somebody else wanted me to be. I don't beat myself up any more about having to be perfect. If it's not perfect it's okay. I know that everything is perfect just the way it is.

The world is my oyster and I'm excited about what's going to happen next. Sometimes I don't know what's going to happen next but it doesn't matter because whatever happens will be for the best. It will lead me to something even greater.

I want people who read my story to know that if you have the opportunity to work with LSL it is going to make your life amazing. No matter how good your life is now it's going to make it even better. Vikki and Nate are very inspirational people. If you're skeptical about working with LSL just do it. It feels like the healthy community that everyone wants.

Thank You
Vicki W

Confidence

Pre LSL

I was working as a Senior Manager in a major financial company in the UK. I was working extremely long hours, constantly stressed and being bullied by an aggressive employee. On the outside I came across as confident, energetic and together. Inside, I was crippled with lack of confidence and a fear of talking to new people and had a tendency to say yes even if I really wanted to say no.

I was always conscious of what people would say about me and I felt like an outsider who never fitted in which made me a real people pleaser who was unwilling to say no. I was unwilling to ask for help because I saw it as a sign of weakness.

I once walked out of a formal black tie dinner because I had been placed on a table with people I didn't know and I simply couldn't cope. I didn't know what to say to them and had a panic attack. I wouldn't return calls from concerned friends for well over a week.

I started working with LSL in 2007 initially to help me overcome the challenges of my lack of confidence.

Relationships

I was just at the start of what was, I can now see, an emotionally abusive relationship with a controlling man. In the early days he ordered me back from a training course in the USA supposedly because he was worried he would lose me and loved me too much. Thankfully, I said no to returning home then. In hindsight, with all the work from LSL, I should have said goodbye to him as this was so clearly controlling and manipulative. I felt ashamed that, as a bright successful woman, I was continually being put down and shouted at and living on edge because of his temper. The relationship ended when he cheated at the same time my father had a stroke. According to him, the relationship ending and his behaviour was my fault.

LSL and Vikki's coaching helped me through this period and to see the relationship for what it was and deal with the emotional fall out from the cheating and the way it ended.

Fast forward 10 years

Business - I have now been a self-employed consultant for 10 years and my confidence in my own knowledge and expertise is so much stronger.

Confidence – I no longer worry about what people think about me and only value peoples opinions if they matter to me. I am much more authentic in showing who I am in a more honest and open way. I may not feel like I fit in all the time but I can honestly say it doesn't worry me now. I'm confident in myself. I am happy sitting at a table with people I don't know as well as sitting on my own.

I'm happy to say no to people now and not feel I should do something in case people don't think I'm nice which is a big step forward for me. I have more confidence in trusting my gut instinct now and it always tends to have the right answer rather than the logical brain talk

I bounce back from set backs within hours rather than the days and weeks it had been before LSL. I also ask for help a lot quicker now. I just wish Id been working with Vikki earlier in my life as who knows where I would be now.

9

I Turned Around One Day

The Lotus Seed Life is an amazing process to go through. For me, the changes were cumulative and I didn't notice them along the way. I turned round one day and I had lost weight, was out dancing every week and genuinely enjoying life.

I first turned to Gill at Lotus Seed Life because I was overweight, single and unhappy. After a few sessions, all of a sudden it was easy to control my eating and I went on to lose 3.5 stones in a year. I also met and fell in love with a lovely man who suits me so well. We have been together for over five years now and are about to be married!

During the process, I was hit with a number of life challenges including the death of my grandmother and the loss of my job. Gill helped me navigate these, process the grief healthily and move on. I have a tendency to get stuck in a rut so the Lotus Seed process at this point in my life was invaluable.

The process itself might feel a little silly - moving your fingers over your forehead and repeating yourself but it does work. Each session is highly personalized to your own circumstances.

I have recently returned to Gill for help processing the grief following the unexpected death of my mother. Once again, I am beginning to see positive ramifications in all aspects of my life.

Thank You
Rachel

Love

When I was growing up, I was told "All men are bastards. Unless they're Indian." Later, as I became a teenager, this was shortened to "All men are bastards." It wasn't just men that were at fault, and they were not all equally at fault. Muslims were thought to be the worst kind of men that existed, because….actually, I forget why. But anyway, I was educated very early on that "English girls are tarts." Unfortunately this separated me from all of my classmates since they were all English girls. It was hard not to be judgmental. This was coupled with the fact that, from a very young age, I was told I was clever by my parents, but then it seemed to change gradually as I didn't develop the particular skills they wanted me to have, namely in science and mathematics. I was more driven towards the arts, English and anything creative. Since this was outside their understanding, my talents were completely overlooked and they stopped telling me how clever I was. As a teenager I noticed people started to remark on how pretty I was, so I decided to focus on that to get male attention.

At the time, I was 28 years old, beautiful, and married to the guy I wanted so badly. I have my own business and a full-time job. I live in central London in a cool flat. I should be happy. I have it all. I'm not. I feel alone, unattractive, undesirable and poor. But what can I do? Nobody takes my quest for help seriously. Everyone thinks I am feeling sorry for myself. "How can you have money problems?" "Money comes in and goes out for you like for nobody else," and "Everybody loves you. Boys want to be with you and girls want to be like you" and "poor little rich girl." These were all statements I was familiar with. When I complained about my job for which I was well qualified I was asked "Did you cheat on your degree?" No one, not even myself, could figure my unhappiness out.

Until I looked deeper, that is. I had gone into my marriage knowing that he was gay, or at least bisexual. During the period from which we met, I went from hearing statements from friends such as "If you want to fit a square shape into a round hole, then go ahead." Later when we were engaged they said "It takes a strong woman to marry him." I was famous for being the woman that was so amazing she could turn a gay man straight. Yet, this outward, so called, validation failed to satisfy me in the long term. Although married me, he was not there all the time. What I mean is, he went from being committed to me and our life together to deciding to leave me to pursue a life of sexual exploration in just one day. It was like being on a roller coaster in the dark because I couldn't see where the track was going.

This unknowing had become a way of life for me and when things were going smoothly, it was easy for me to put negative thoughts to the back of mind. It was on one of these happy evenings that I met Armand at a business networking event. He was there not to promote his own business but to promote someone else he and his girlfriend had been working with. He told me that his girlfriend had had depression for 20 years when she started working with Vikki, a kind of life coach, over the phone, doing a new technique that I had never heard of. He said that she got over the depression within a few months and now she was happy. They were happy. Well, I wasn't depressed, I was fully functional, so I thought to myself that if the Lotus Seed Life can do that much for a formerly depressed person, then imagine how happy I could be!

Armand gave me a US phone number for this lady he told me about and I called a few days later. I was nervous about calling a stranger so far away on the other side of the Atlantic, in a state I had never visited. *"What will she think of me, will she want to work with me, maybe I'm just too bad for her to work with."* All these thoughts were going around in my head as I left a message on her voicemail. I waited for her to call back, she didn't, so I called again. At the end of the call she said, "I need to tell you a secret, the way it works is that I can't call you, you must call me, because you have to ask for help for it to work."

We decided to work together. I told her a bit about myself, that I had got married but that I didn't seem to be doing or accomplishing what I had always wanted to do, that I felt I was failing at life. She listened and I felt I could trust her. It felt like, for the first time, I wasn't being judged for what was making me unhappy. Someone finally understood what it was like to be me. This freed me up to tell her more. The more I opened up, the more she could help me. I used to call her on the way to work when I was down. She would uplift me and I was ready to face the day.

Then one day, my husband decided to leave for good. I was devastated but Vikki supported me to leave the flat immediately because I could not afford to live there on my own. By the end of the week I had packed up and left London. I was staying with my parents, not something I wanted to do at the time, but I knew it was the best option so I got on with it. What followed was a journey of job searching, soul searching and finding my voice. During this period my husband and I tried to get back together but stayed separated. The work I did with LSL helped me to draw the line and not to take him back on a whim, but to give him space and to let myself have some time, too. Personal time was something I had never done before. I got into a relationship with him three months after ending another serious relationship. Resisting getting back together with him was hard, but doing the LSL techniques with Vikki helped me to see the patterns of monogamy I had created, I created patterns of being dependent and not believing that I was complete as a single unit; needing someone to validate me so I could feel good enough to be loved.

I started to appreciate my own company, to recognize my talents and my self-worth. It was because of this I learned to draw the line. When it came down to us to decide whether to divorce or get back together, I wanted a divorce. I finally realized that this was not the end of my life, but that I had a chance to make a bigger, better life without him by my side. I could find someone who appreciated me, who I could love fully and who would love me back and if I didn't find him, it didn't matter.

When I realized this, things started to change for me. I started my own business, backed by my family who had not approved of my marriage, and were totally behind the divorce. It took time for things to unravel themselves and I was single for over two years before I met someone new. In that time I had fun, I met new people, traveled, visited Vikki many times and learned to be an empowered independent woman who does not need a man to be happy.

I no longer need reassurance all the time and have a strong self-belief and sense of self-worth. People can say anything to me and I am unaffected. As for the ex-husband, we are no longer in touch but I wish him well.

Before doing LSL, even though I had the dream of meeting my ideal guy, I had no concept of what that really meant. I thought it meant meeting some rich guy, European or American who was perfect in every way. He had to be drop dead gorgeous, socially acceptable and classy. During the process of doing the LSL, this all changed and I vowed to myself that the only reason ever to get married was for love. I guess before I did LSL, I didn't really know what love was or how I would recognize it. I didn't even believe it really existed. I had mistaken guys falling over themselves to be with me for love, and me falling over guys being overwhelming love. Now, with new insight, I knew that it was just a lack of self-esteem and having changed those patterns, I was free to create new concepts on love and new ideas and beliefs.

I decided I wanted my future husband to be kind. That was it.

One day, long after my first marriage was over, it was January and I was in a bit of a social rut. When my parents asked if I wanted to go out to an Indian folk festival event I accepted. As we walked into a spacious yet empty hall that night, musicians were setting up and people were entering in their brightly colored clothes. We found a table of my parents' friends and sat down. Shortly afterwards a live band started and out of the corner of the room. A singer emerged, holding a microphone. His tone was deep and affecting. His voice seemed larger than the hall that was carrying it. I was overwhelmed as if some star had just walked in. I looked over at him and our eyes met. He was tall, dark and handsome with shoulder length hair. He wore a black turtleneck and a jacket with black jeans. He continued to sing. It felt like I was walking on air. He serenaded our table and was so smooth I was convinced he did this with all the women every night. Later we danced together and he asked for my number. I gave it to him discretely as I knew my parents wouldn't be too chuffed about me flirting with a singer.

I didn't pick up when he called me an hour later. I knew the so-called rules about taking a booty call. The next day I was at work and when I looked at my phone there were several missed calls and messages from him. I didn't call. It was two or three days later that I finally answered the phone. I was reluctant to meet him. Partly because I didn't know anything about him but also, his English wasn't very good, and to me he obviously didn't understand the protocol of dating. He was also Muslim. While talking to Vikki she helped me see that I was judging him from my expectations of how it should go. I was judging him based on my parents beliefs about men and about Muslims. I wasn't giving him the chance to be him and getting to know him as he is, rather I had an idea of how I should be treated in a relationship and what that ought to look like.

    The other doubt in my mind was that he was a singer on a work permit. I knew my parents, both full time doctors, would not approve. My mum said "he's not responsible." I reminded her that he works six nights a week "if that's not responsible, then what is?" But his work ethic wasn't the real issue. The main thing bothering everyone was he was a Muslim and he was from Pakistan. Okay so, not only was I dating a man, who are, based on my upbringing, supposedly all bastards, he was also the worst kind of man, a Muslim one. If I had not worked with the LSL when I met him, I would have rebelled with anger at my family's disapproval. I would've stopped dating him. Instead, I was advised to tell them about Navi step by step; one week at a time, and that's what I did. Each week I told them something new about him. I didn't get angry. I answered their questions calmly.

    The process of applying for his visa to stay in the UK took over two years during which time we were physically separated, linked only by phone since he didn't have Wi-Fi at home. During this time I lost my job. Things were not great with my family but, thanks to my work with LSL, I was strong. I had faith in our love and belief in our actions and our dreams of starting a family together. Without the inner strength that I found while doing LSL, I may have been distracted and side-tracked by my parents and other people. Then I would have blamed it on him for being away, being a "typical man" and not caring even though he was in a helpless situation. I may have given up on the greatest love of my life. As it was however, we didn't doubt each other even once. He consistently called me when he said he would and several times a day when he hadn't said he would. He was always loving and the things we talked about as well as the distance between us made our love grow stronger.

Our endurance paid off, his visa came through, Navi came back to the UK and we moved in together. I calmly told my parents that we would be getting married and starting our life together. They were not happy but they had to accept it because I wasn't arguing.

We got on with our new life. He turned out to be kind in so many ways. He treated me with respect right from the start. By respect I don't necessarily mean talking politely or holding the door for me or buying me dinner which is what I thought it meant before. It went much deeper than that. He was interested in finding out about me; what I was interested in, what made me tick and that was new in my life. People say that all couples argue but we don't. We have discussions. We accept what the other is saying and take it into consideration even though we each have strong opinions. Our relationship goes beyond my old limitations of how great a relationship could be.

My parents were watching all this from a distance and it didn't take long for them to realize that he was a good man who treated their daughter well and with respect. They soon came around and they invited us over for Christmas. Now they dote on their son-in-law and they make sure they have all his favorite foods ready whenever we visit. I am thankful that I did not react when my parents were disapproving or carry any anger into the relationship or it would not be the thriving loving union that it is today.

We were so happy the day we found out I was pregnant. We sat down on the bed and hugged. It took a few days for it to sink in. Our families were overjoyed when they heard. It was an easy pregnancy thanks to the LSL work I had done. I accepted being pregnant, being a mother and being viewed as "old" by my children! When he finally came through and we took one look at the baby, our lives changed forever. I felt such a whoosh of overwhelming unconditional love.

Since Yani was little I parented by intuition as mothers have been doing forever. Of course, I was also working it out as I went along but the difference was that we were coming from our intuition, doing what felt right in our gut. That's what a lot of parents are not able to do because they haven't developed themselves sufficiently to be able to cast aside what other people say about how they should live their lives and how parenting should be done. So, they fall into the trap of doing what they are told. The very concept that every child is the same and should be disciplined in the same way to me is crazy. Every child is unique. Every parent is unique. I leaned to follow my instincts a long time ago, well before Yani was born and I'm glad I did because if I hadn't I don't know where I would be now.

Yani is his own person. If I listened to what others said I should be doing, I would probably feel like a failure as a mother, even though I know I am a good one. If I did do what I was supposed to, I would again be pushing a square shape (Yani) through a round hole by trying to make him something he is not. We want to nurture and bring out the best in him and the way to do that is to discipline him in ways that empower him.

The thing with the LSL is that what I learned about myself can be applied to all sorts of different situations. For me, it was parenting. I have enough self-belief to know that I am good mother despite doing things differently.

A great example is that as soon as Yani turned 3 years old, everybody said "You have to get a balance bike, it's the latest thing, it's the only way they learn balance, stabilisers don't help." I was tempted of course, everyone was saying it, so maybe it was true. Even so, my husband and I decided we wouldn't get a balance bike, we'd get a normal bike with stabilizers. So that's what we got him and he rode it happily for a year. In that time, while we were out on his bike, other children came along past us on their balance bikes. We said "hello" and carried on our way. Then, one Sunday, I thought he was ready so I got out the screwdriver and off came the stabilizers. We took him to a park with a hill. We pushed him gently down a small grassy hill without the stabilizers. He fell over a few times, but he stayed upright more often than not. Then we held on to the back of his bike while he rode around the park and when he wasn't looking, let go of him. Before he knew it, he was riding by himself on two wheels! All this with no balance bike needed. Our son is the first in his year group to ride a bike. He started his first day of school by riding his two-wheeler pedal bike while all the other children were still scooting. All the parents were looking at us, saying, "Wow, look at that little boy riding his two-wheeler bike, that's amazing. How did he learn so quickly?"

I'm not invalidating balance bikes, of course they have their place and for some children they obviously work. My point is that following our instincts really paid off and I'm glad that I had children after doing the LSL because I enjoy being a parent much more that I would have if I had done it the other way around. When I had loads of stuff going on in my head; feeling guilty; blaming other people; thinking about things that could go wrong all the time I would have driven myself crazy with doubt. I would have transferred all this stuff onto Yani and, inevitably, I would have thought it was all his fault I was feeling this way. Consequently, he would have been a very different child. Thankfully, I did do the LSL work before becoming a mother. I am proud to say that Yani is a very happy, balanced child who has a lot of confidence. He says "hello" to other children and adults even if he doesn't know them. He is very active and wants to try new things. If I was still the angry and uptight person that I was he would have felt that and absorbed it like a sponge, probably developing into an angry adolescent and teenager. But now, my mind is free to think about what's best for him while also taking care of myself. What other people think is of no consequence to the three of us. I am now having my second child with the most loving and attentive husband a girl could ask for. He appreciates and loves me as I do him. We have a wonderful, respectful, fulfilling relationship because we are fulfilled in ourselves.

Thank you LSL

Supi, Navi, Yani, and baby

I Know What I Want

All I really want to say is. . .don't knock it till you try it! But try it, what do you have to lose?

I have been lucky enough to work with the Lotus Seed Life for quite some time. I am a totally different person than I was before I started working with LSL.

As a child I was very emotionally suppressed. I was brought up by what I call a church cult. I can count on one hand how me times I had cried in my life. Then, one day, when I was 28 I started crying and all my motions came out. It was only in October/November 2012 when I was diagnosed with depression. Looking back I can see I had been suffering from it for many years. I had a terrible breakup. A dear friend of mine passed away. I didn't have a relationship with my parents.

For many that know me I seemed like the opposite of someone who would have depression but, in late 2012, it really affected me in all levels. I'm still not sure exactly why in September/October it was triggered but I think it was a number of things over the years that contributed it to come out in a very dramatic way.

I had been feeling quite down for a while and just assumed I would snap out of it eventually but the feelings kept getting worse. I became very very emotional, lost my appetite, therefore lost quite a lot of weight, lost all motivation for any thing, just wanted to sleep all the time but then struggled with that too. I just wanted to hide and not see anyone. As I wasn't eating properly it started to affect me in all areas. Things I loved like training and meeting friends was a challenge. Because I wasn't eating I had no energy to train. I knew I would be deficient in nutrients therefore would feel down even more. Permanently feeling drained really affected my personality. I knew I needed to try and eat as it would help me feel better so I would try to force feed myself. Just eating wasn't really dealing with the issues. The worst part of the experience was the panic attacks I was getting. I was having about 5-10 per day and I just couldn't handle it.

  By the end of November I still couldn't get out of this low and I was desperate. It had been two or so months without any improvement. I knew it was serious and I needed to do something drastic but wasn't sure what to do. I decided to go to my GP and see what they could offer... Without doing any tests the doctor said I needed to go on anti depressants. I was shocked that was the first thing they recommended. I asked if there were any alternatives. They offered counseling but it wasn't available till January and I urgently needed help right then. Coming from a health and fitness background, I knew there must be more natural alternatives. I had tried supplementation but it wasn't working at the time. I looked at counseling options as I had heard of a few things.

  Back in May 2012 I went to a strength workshop and seminar at Tom Hibbert's Winning Health Solutions in Southampton. At the end of the day he spoke about something he had used for his mental health and that he had had great results. It was called the Lotus Seed life (LSL). He spoke shortly about it and recommended it. I was really interested at the time and took the leaflet and then put it to the back of my mind. So when I was desperate in November I got in touch with Tom to ask a little bit more about it. He said it's not for everyone but there's no harm in having a trial session.

I got in touch with LSL and had a trial session over the phone with Vikki during which I gave my background and why I needed help. Then three days later I had a follow up session where I decided that I was going to give the process a try. I was put in touch with Gill and we began sessions. The LSL works on a concept of the sub conscious mind. We would go through a certain topic such as 'confidence' and talk through the negatives then plant the positives in my mind. We'd do a new session every three to four days which gave my mind time to process the work. The first 3/4months were really tough and we worked on some deep subjects. By January and February I was a lot better. I was having a lot less panic attacks and able to get out of my lows a lot quicker.

I have been consistently doing the sessions for a while and have improved dramatically. I feel I'm really going in the right direction. Don't get me wrong, I still get my low days but I've improved so much that I couldn't be happier with the progress.

I have a better relationship with my family now that I'm able to openly communicate. I know what I want. I know where I want to go with business and in my personal life. I'm living and loving life more than I could have ever imagined. It may take a few months before you see a huge change, it did for me. But with each session, I felt calmer, more stable, and less scattered. As time went on, the more sessions I did, the more confident, empowered I felt. Anxiety is gone. I am financially better off. I am finally me and proud of it.

My business is going great, my clientele is growing. I can now confidently say that I am a successful personal trainer. I am training to be an LSL associate. I want to help my clientele like I was helped.

Thank you for reading this,
Grace Brown

My Right to Live

Please be warned that, while this story has a happy ending, it is graphic in nature and contains sexual and violent content.

Writing my life story has been difficult but a learning experience. Here is what I have pieced together and found out over the years. I certainly hope that some of you will identify with the abuse that I suffered and do something to put it behind you. Lotus Seed Life (LSL) has helped me put it behind me.

Let's start with a little background. My family consists of 5 children and my parents. My twin brother is the oldest of 5, he was born one full hour before me. I almost didn't make it due to all of the beatings that my dad gave my mom, even during pregnancy.

One of my earliest memories is when my brother and I were 7. My siblings were 5, 3, and 18 months old. At this time my father was in prison for living off immoral earnings (he was my mother's pimp). My mom was "on the game" meaning she was his prostitute. He intimidated her with the fear of more beatings if she didn't perform and bring in money.

On this particular day I remember my brother and I coming home from school and our neighbor was watching the younger kids while my mom was out working. The neighbor brought the younger kids back to our house so that my brother and I could watch them. The neighbor saw that my mom wasn't home and called social services. The police came and took us away. They put us on the "at risk register" and gave us a social worker. This was the beginning of my siblings and I being split up, and back together, split up and back together many times over the course of our childhood. We went from foster home to foster home, and from children's home to children's home.

One time I remember sticking up for myself with my mom, she hit me and hit me. She beat me pretty bad. From that time on I learned to do what I was told and to never question anything.

Another memory I have is when we were all back together. My dad took all of us kids out of England to another country that didn't speak English. My father had an agenda and a reason to do this. We were told it was to start a new life, but I don't think that was true. My dad's mom took care of us but she was very mean. She would lock us in the closet for weeks at a time. It didn't matter what we did it it was never good enough. She would beat us until we had welts. She would beat us regularly. My mom flew out from England to get us and take us home. She couldn't take all of us at once because she didn't have the money. So my mom took the youngest siblings back to England. My dad was supposed to send us older kids back to England later but he didn't.

At the time I was 13. My mother was gone. My father started molesting me. He told me it was to teach me how to please boys. He would do different things to me sexually. He would have me do things on him to "teach" me. If I didn't do the right, I would get hit. He taught me to masturbate while he watched, telling me it was for my own good. Everything is for my own good. I was afraid not to do these things.

One day a lady came and talked to my dad. This lady took the boys and put them in a home run by a priest. They put me in a convent. I thought it was because my parents were split up. But I have my doubts. I really think it was because my father didn't want us.

The convent was a terrible place. In the convent not many people spoke English. I was constantly ridiculed for my accent. I was put down for everything I did. In the convent the kids did all the work. We washed the windows, we did the dishes, we scrubbed the floors, we cleaned the bathrooms. We did it all. If it wasn't done well, we got punished. We were punished all the time for something. One of the punishments was we were put in isolation which was a very very small dark damp room. We were often hit with anything that nuns had handy, a stick, a pipe, a cane, or their hand. These punishments were often unspeakable. We slept on the floor. We took cold showers. If we didn't eat all that they gave us, then we didn't eat for three days. We had to buy our own toothpaste and soap and personal things with our own money. I never got any money from my parents so I had to borrow beg or steal things, or just go without. I remember one of the nuns screaming at me "you're so fat and disgusting no one will have you and you will be here for the rest of your life!" The next day I wrote a letter to my dad and gave it to a friend at school to mail. I knew that the nuns read all of our mail. In the letter I begged him to come and get me out of this terrible place. I was so scared of being tortured the rest of my life. It took him some time but eventually he got me out. I was 15 at the time. A couple of years later my mom got the boys out.

Between the ages of 15 and 17 I got into drugs. Mostly LSD(acid). I lived with my dad and his new prostitute wife until she gave my dad an ultimatum of either getting rid of me or her leaving. He chose her. I remember I was coming down off acid when my dad introduced me to these two "nice" men. I thought he was arranging a place for me to live but when I got there I was gang raped by 10 men. I think it was 10 but I lost count. Once they were done with me I was discarded like trash. I was thrown back to the streets. I knew then that my dad had sold me. I left and I was living on the street. I did for most of my teenage years.

I went from bad relationship to bad relationship. I was very naïve but I did what I was told. One of my boyfriends beat me up constantly. One time he beat me so bad he broke my nose and my eyes got all swollen. He wouldn't let me go to the doctor. He told me it was for my own good. A couple of days later he told me he was dying. He told me he didn't didn't want me to have to go through that so he left me. The truth was he had another girlfriend and he didn't want me anymore.

I met a member of the Buddhist congregation and I fell in love. I became a Buddhist. When I was about 19 years old we got married and we had 3 children. That relationship lasted about six years. He remarried shortly after the divorce. His new wife didn't want anything to do with my children. My kids hardly saw their father. After few years of being on my own I met a man and married him. But I didn't love him. I needed him to help support me and the kids. He was mean to the kids and me. I thought it was normal. After all everyone in my life had beat me. The boys were 17, 15 and 12 when we got divorced.

I have suffered from severe PMS all of my life. During those times of the month I often got angry. I would shout and even hit the kids when they were younger. Because of the PMS I was depressed and hopeless. I continued to handle and manage situations badly. I had a few short-term relationships but things didn't get better.

My father was probably beat by his mother, so he beat my mother and us kids. My mother was beat by my father, and so beat us kids. I was beat by my parents, so I hit my kids. The cycle goes on.
When I was 32 I had a hysterectomy and died on the operating table. They managed to resuscitate me. I also suffered from a prolapsed bladder during that operation. I now suffered from

fibromyalgia.

In my 40's I came out as a lesbian. This brought on a whole host of new challenges. When I came out I wrote my father letter asking him how could he have been so mean to me. I asked how could he have hurt me so badly; how could he have discarded me. I got no reply. Later when he was on his deathbed I went to see him. All he said to me was "I probably shouldn't have done what I did, but I did so live with it. You deserved it."

I thought after admitting I was a lesbian my life would get easier. I got into a relationship with another woman. That relationship lasted 8 ½ years. She was unfaithful but at least she didn't beat me. There was a silver lining.

When we ended it I was on antidepressants. I was feeling dysfunctional and figured I was really broken. I let people walk all over me and I never stood up for myself. I did everything I was always told. I felt unwanted. I was never good enough. My life was not my own.

I joined and belong to a positive living group. One night they had a guest speaker named Geoff Sober. He talked about Lotus Seed Life and how it helps change your mindset. It makes changes in your life for the better. I liked what he had to say and thought I'd give it a go.

If you do judge me or feel sorry for me I won't take it personally. LSL has taught me that I did what I had to do to survive. LSL has taught me the things I did, I did because I didn't know any better. I have learned to forgive myself and others. I have learned to love myself. I have learned that I deserve respect. I am finally calm and in control of my life. I am finally free of my abuse cycle. Life experiences have shown me I have a fighting soul. Now with LSL I have the empowerment, courage and ability to fight for my God-given right; the right to be respected, honored, and loved in a kind caring fashion.

With the support of LSL I now have loving relationships with my children my mother and everyone in my life.

I would recommend LSL to everyone and anyone who wants to resolve their issues and get out of their cycles. LSL works with every aspect of a person's life. I am stronger, more courageous and living with hope in my future because of LSL. I'm happier than I have ever been before. I have the confidence to deal with every situation in a positive way. I stand up for me. I speak my mind freely and calmly. I have come to terms with and let go of my past. I am finally me and proud of it.

I would like to thank Vikki Faudel and Gill Wright for all of the love, the support, the knowledge they have shown me through my incredible journey. Working with LSL has changed my life and my relationships. Thank you for saving me.

Thank you
Anonymous

Poem: Who am I?

I am an adult

but I am a child

I have 2 brothers and one sister

but I have at least 6 sets of parents

people call me their friend

but I only have one friend

I have what everyone wants

but I don't have me

I am free

but I don't have my freedom

I have lights

but I am in the dark

I do no wrong

yet I do nothing right

everyone tells me what to do

but I have no say in what I do

I never say no

but to myself

I trust everyone

but no one trust me

I never hurt

but I get hurt

I am heard

but never listen to

I see

but I am not seen

I make people happy

but I have never seen happiness

I care about everyone

but who cares about me

I love

but in my loved

I am _____

but who am I

Written by anonymous: pertains to everyone!

Resolving Old Conflicts

My Lotus Seed Life (LSL) journey has been one of tremendous transformation.

I started my personal development many years ago. I read self-help books, attended seminars, and was doing all I could to change my patterns and better my life. I was a self-help junkie. One of the many seminars I attended was on Emotional Freedom Technique (EFT). EFT helps release people's stuff and blockages by tapping reflexology points throughout the body. I made what I thought were some positive changes. At one point I was clearing so many of my blocks and issues I thought I would have permanent dents in my face from all the tapping.

I was so excited by the changes I had made that I trained to be an EFT practitioner. I also trained as a life coach. After completing both trainings, I left my job and set up my own coaching business. I felt happier and I knew, in theory, how to have a better life. The problem is it isn't always easy to turn the theory into a reality. A lot of seminars and self-help books are great while you're reading them or attending them yet, when you get back to your daily life, they don't work.

One day the EFT trainer introduced me to Vikki and LSL. I wasn't sure what to think of this. I trusted him but I still felt a bit weird. In the beginning I couldn't pinpoint any specific changes but after some time passed I began to see my patterns changing.

Let me explain:

Past Relationships:

My relationships all had similar attributes. I was in a unhappy relationships with men who didn't communicate with me. They made everything out to be my fault. A lot of the times they were afraid of commitment. They often cheated on me. I was often criticized, bullied, and made to feel that I wasn't worth much. I've had a lot of people tell me what I should and shouldn't do. I have tried to turn myself inside out so they would like me. They have tried to make me feel guilty and question myself on how I could be better for them.

Past Career:

When I was younger my dream was to be on stage or on TV. One of my earliest memories is playing in the streets outside my house and imagining myself being a great actress. I even fought with my parents to let me do a one year drama and dance course. After the course was finished, my parents wanted me to "get a normal job." My parents couldn't wrap their heads around the idea of me wanting to be in front of the camera.

My relationship with my parents:

For many years my relationship with my parents and family had been very challenging. I felt like an outsider. I felt like they didn't understand me. I was the solo extrovert in a family of introverts. My parents could be quite critical, especially my mom.

My Past Stuff:

I had a lot of negative beliefs. I believed I wasn't good enough. I believed I wasn't worthy of the best. I didn't have the confidence to be a professional actor. I was doing all the work in my relationships. I questioned myself constantly. I often over ate to stuff down my emotions. I justified my drinking by saying I was having fun when I actually drank to drown out my feelings. I couldn't even have silence in the house because my negative thoughts were so overwhelming. I binged on chocolates and biscuits and chips. After a binge I felt physically ill and emotionally down. I felt guilty. Then the cycle would start all over again.

After working with LSL and with the support and guidance and doing sessions with Vikki my life changed in ways I can't even begin to communicate. Some of the changes are subtle and sometimes they are immediate but one thing is for sure, they are all very impactful and powerful and get results.

Current Relationship:

I got out of my unhappy marriage long before I met Vikki or LSL. However, after LSL I stopped attracting men who were not good for me.

I'm engaged to be married to a wonderful man. His name is Steve. (His story starts on page ___.) He treats me like a queen. He is supportive of my business and my acting career. He is attentive and generous and we've been together in this fantastic loving relationship since 2009. I know that I now deserve the love and romance of a good man and that man is Steve. He is so wonderful that he has been working with LSL as well. I can't say enough wonderful things about him I love him for who he is. He loves me for who I am. Our relationship is one of mutual trust and respect honest communication and support.

Current Career:

In addition to my business coaching creative business onwers, I am now also a professional actor. I have been cast in a play, asked to sing a demo CD for a new musical, and enrolled in acting classes. The LSL sessions helped me to get out of my own way. I have appeared twice in the UK's longest running and much loved TV series *Coronation Street*. I've been in numerous short films and independent feature films. I have been paid for different acting gigs. I am so grateful to LSL for helping me embrace my creative self and express who I am.

My relationship with my parents:

Both my parents passed away a couple of years ago. I was so grateful that our conflicts had been resolved while they were still alive. I was able to love and accept them for who they were. I could see that they loved me in their own way and was able to release the years of hurt and pain that I had perceived. Unfortunately, my mom didn't get to see me on *Coronation Street* but my dad did. He was so excited, and I was excited to see his excitement at doing what I love.

My Current Stuff:

I have gotten rid of the negative chatter and beliefs about myself. I have been able to recognize and deal with my lessons. I am more confident. I am an actor and I love it. I eat healthy. I take care of myself. My old negative patterns and cycles are gone.

Having done LSL, negative stuff now stands out like coal on white snow. I believe in myself now. I have no doubt that without LSL or Vikki, I would not be as happy as I am in my career, my wonderful relationship and in myself.

If you have the opportunity to work with LSL make it happen. Don't hesitate to pick up the phone today. If you have the chance to go to Denver to go any of the LSL retreats, go!

My fiancé and I got to go in 2016. It meant a lot that he was able to go with me. It was an amazing adventure for both of us. It helped us grow individually and together. You never know what's will happen on the retreats. You might be engaged in a water fight in the house. You might have to jump off a rock into a river. One thing is for sure, it will be amazing. The love and acceptance that Vikki, Nate, and their daughters share with you is indescribable. You will learn to be yourself to have fun and feel a real community and a sense of belonging.

I want to thank Vikki, Nate, Samantha and Jackie (their daughters), and the entire LSL team.

Una Doyle-Love

Forgiving to Move On

I recall thinking to myself it would be waste of time talking to "this Vikki." The conversation would just be like all the other conversations that I had over past few years. I really did not want to call Vikki as I had had a traumatic long weekend. I had a chicken bone stuck in my throat and spent three days in hospital with the possibility of throat surgery to extract the bone. Besides, I had already spoken to an array of therapists face to face who just talked with me. Talk, talk, talk. They could not help me with the past or coping with the ongoing situation. So how would someone thousands of miles in the States even begin to help me here in the UK? But I made the call as I would have been embarrassed as Tom Hibbert, my new personal trainer, had written the introduction e-mail and I had arranged a time to speak with her.

I was so wrong. Vikki has turned my life and my partner's life around for the better. She saved us from self-destruction. I do not exaggerate my feelings and words as my situation was extreme. I am scientifically trained so everything, for me, is proven by fact. I need proof. Lotus Seed Life (LSL) has done what many of the mainstream specialist therapists could not do for me; help me manage and cope with the my life.

The past seven years have been difficult in relation to my employment and family. I resigned from a good, well paid job under constructive dismissal. I was taking the company I worked for to an employment tribunal. This was emotionally draining as I had to re-live the awful situations in the workplace. After a year of aggressive letters between the employer and solicitors a conclusion was reached without having to go to court. I was left completely destroyed with no self-esteem, I lacked confidence, I felt no self-belief or self-worth.

Four months prior, both my elderly parents had fallen ill. Dad had terminal prostate cancer and was not given long to live. My mum had a mini stroke and dementia. When one came out of hospital the other went into hospital. My mom had forgotten how to walk. It was difficult to acknowledge that both my parents were so ill.

My dad had mellowed over the years. Growing up, he had been very strict, controlling and an emotionally abusive person. He was now a calmer more forgiving man but the cancer reverted him back to his old ways. My parents and brother did not want me to get stressed out with their situation as I have a stress relate illness, eczema. My brother took more and more control of my parents affairs.

I had always protected my mum from everything I could. She accepted being treated badly and abused by my dad, his family, her own brothers, and even her own son. Even as a child, I would get between her and dad to stop the abuse. I got the slipper, the ruler, the belt as punishment. This was normal for me. Mum and I would both cry together due to, what I now know. was emotional abuse. There would be an uproar at the smallest thing such as the wrong sized fork for dinner. This was my childhood.

My skin is a true reflection of the stress in my life. At one point in my life, I could not even walk down the stairs. I had to go down on my bottom and crawl up because my skin hurt so much. As you may know, children of abusers often become the abuser themselves. My brother has a horrible temper. On one occasion my brother had me on the floor with a pair of scissors to my throat.

I had shouted at him for marking up my freelance work that was going to be published in a scientific journal. I was on the floor. My dad did not help me. My mum tried but my brother was too strong. He finally let go. A few days later he left for the Far East. While he was there he took lots of money from my family. After some time passed my brother came home.

My mum called dad's angry fits of rage and abuse his "moods." These moods would often ruin special occasions or times with friends and family functions. I remember my parents' 50th wedding anniversary. I was so excited for my both my mum and dad. Sadly, my dad ruined the day with one of his moods even though we kept it low-key. A couple of days later his mood was still full of anger when my partner and I went to visit them. My partner left my parents' house before me because he did not like how my dad was treating my mum. He watched dad thump mum on the back and she lost her stability. I lost my temper for the first time in my life with my dad that day. I shouted at him. Dad was placing my mum at risk of a fall. I told him that he was a bully. For the first time in my mom's life, she agreed with me. My brother came screaming into the room. As he pulled me away from my dad, my dad fell backwards pushing my mum over. She hit her head on a table. I was told to leave and never come back to their home again.

Two weeks later the police visited me at home. My brother reported me for assault on my mum. He told them that I had pushed my mum over which caused a serious head injury resulting in several visits to hospital. I was overwhelmed at how the facts of that day had been changed. I told the police everything; the truth.

I received a lengthy letter from a solicitor representing my parents and brother. This was a letter filled with lies and extreme accusations against me. The letter stated that I nearly killed my dad by strangling him and caused him to nearly have a heart attack.

The letter stipulated that in order for me to see my mum again, I had to agree that I had done all of which I had been accused. I could not. In addition, I had to undergo an exorcism. I made an appointment with my priest who confirmed that I was not possessed and no exorcism was going to be performed. My priest gave me the blessing of a sacrament. This is was good not enough for my brother. My brother had become the main abuser in the household.

Months passed and I was not allowed to see or speak with my mum. Once, I managed to speak with mum for a few minutes but the phone went dead. I later had the police at my home because of the call. My brother reported me. Due to all the stress, I fell seriously ill and was taken into hospital. My partner called my parents and left a message. He tried calling my brother and was subjected to verbal abuse. He then went to my parents' house to try to speak with them. Again, he was met with verbal abuse. My parents were nowhere to be seen. The porch door was slammed on my partner's hand.

I soon realized that my whole family on both sides had cut me off. They believed the lies about me. The family would not even listen to me or view my factual proof. (My partner had recordings of my brother's verbal abuse.)

I was always taking chances to see my parents. I would often sneak over to their house. I was greeted by abuse from my brother. One day my dad opened the door and spoke for a couple of hours. My brother was in Scotland. My brother installed CCTV so that he could watch remotely to keep me away and ensure my parents did as they were told. My parents had daily Skype calls with him. One day he called and he made my dad do a 360 degrees with the lap top to ensure that there was no one in the house. My dad told me to hide. During the ten days I had with my parents, I started to disprove all the lies that my brother said about me. My parents began to believe me and listened to my proof.

However on my brother's return the situation reverted back. The abuser stays in control and the victims become powerless again. We had so many encounters like this. The Catholic Church and others did try to help but were unsuccessful.

Several months later I got a call from my uncle in Canada informing me that my dad had passed away five days prior in a hospital three miles from my home. I contacted all the funeral directors in the area to try to find out details of his funeral and eventually found out. I was told that my brother would not permit me to see my dad in the chapel of rest. This was so cruel of my brother. I visited the priest who was conducting the funeral service. My brother told him that under no circumstances was I to be told the date of the funeral. Thankfully, the Catholic priest could not abide by my brother's wishes.

The day of dad's funeral I sat in the front pew with my partner. My brother helped carry the coffin into the church. My mum followed with her brother one side and his wife the other side. Each held my mum by her forearm as if she could not walk. During the service, at the "peace be with you" point, I went over and kissed my mum whispering that I loved her. My partner did the same. That was the last time I touched and spoke to my mum. I never knew that I could cry so much. Subconsciously, I knew I had not only lost my dad that day but my mum as well.

I was distraught and disheartened. I didn't trust anyone, not even my own feelings. I couldn't believe what anyone said. I didn't feel I was good enough to carry on. I started believing I was the problem. I felt as though I was going mad. I had no hope. I was afraid that what I was going through was never going to end. I would never be able to cope. I felt persecuted. I would never be a functioning adult. Maybe, just maybe, I had imagined all the abuse. I had lost my career and my parents. I had lost everything. Because of my mindset, every area of my life seem to be filled with abuse and negativity.

I really wanted to block everything out. A gradual build-up of increasing alcohol and sleeping tablets blanked me out. Eventually this became normal for me.

I did have my partner. He was suffering as he watched me destroy myself. At one point, I told my partner to leave me. I had ruined his life and he needed to find happiness. He was never going to be happy with me in the mess I was in. He had no life staying with me. He never left but stood by me even stronger. He was my rock.

At one point I even went to see a reputable clairvoyant. I thought that she might be able to give me hope. She helped for a day or so but then I was back to my low.

Eventually I started training with a personal trainer near my house. I managed to reduce my daily alcohol to zero. But then my beliefs crept in and I self sabotaged.

A friend recommended Winning Health Solutions. I was nervous. *Was the trainer going to stop my self sabotage? Was the trainer going to be able to see through my issues? Was this going to be like all of the other things I had attracted into my life? Would this be another negative experience to add to the long list of ways I was making myself suffer by choosing things I knew would fail?.* I have learned I was doing all this to play the role of martyr in my own life from Vikki. At the entrance to the gym I stopped and did not want to go in. My partner spent time encouraging me. When we walked into the gym, a big chap with a beard asked if he could help. He had such a gentle voice. We then met Tom Hibbert. I actually felt that something about Tom and his gym was so very different. It was relaxed. It felt like a peaceful and a happy place. I felt safe. My partner was also impressed and felt it was a safe place for me. I am still training with Tom.

My first LSL session was with Tom. At that time, I

believed, and knew that I was beyond help but went along with LSL as I had nothing to lose. I felt physically and mentally lighter after my first session. On my third session I mentioned that I wanted to find someone spiritual to help me. Tom recommended that I speak with Vikki and that she may point me in the best direction. I reluctantly made the call.

Vikki listened to an express version of what had happened in my life; the abuse my parents and I were subjected to and the ongoing situation. She understood that no one wanted to listen to me and that one knew how to help me. No one wanted to help me. I found it difficult to accept that someone thousands of miles away *could* help me. I went with the flow. *What did I have to lose by talking to her?* She appeared to know what was going on in my life by asking me some very specific questions. She did not think I was mad. Most of all, she knew she could help me and she did. In the first conversation, I felt I was really being listened to and that someone actually cared. It was truly an amazing feeling.

Vikki did say that there was a lot of work to be done and asked if I was prepared to work and do the assigned home work. I agreed that I was ready. I recall thinking *how difficult could the homework be?* I was naïve and ignorant. I did not understand how difficult it was going to be. As one who is going through the process I found the emotional highs and lows were sometimes difficult. I was also the one who had to get out of my comfort zone. I was given the homework of buying someone else a cup of coffee. I had to be ready to give up my past, my family, and take control of my life. Vikki is very good at pushing people out of our comfort zones and out of our limiting beliefs and teaching us to take chances, and to live life to the fullest. My partner saw that I was relieved that "this woman" in the States was calming me down. I trusted Vikki which was a major step forward for me. This was the second time I trusted, the first time was Tom.

LSL was financially expensive, especially when I was not

working but we adapted our spending. We are both so pleased and relieved that we made this decision. We could not have spent our money more wisely than by investing in our lives.

   Our house is old. There are always noises that house makes. I slept with the TV and lights on as I suffered from nightmares and night terrors. This seemed normal. When I started LSL, these things heightened. It may sound weird to some reading my story but this is true. I did feel uncomfortable in my home at times. However, I knew Vikki was there for me. I would wake up screaming or sobbing or in a fit (physically thrashing around uncontrollably). One Sunday morning, my partner came home after a night shift and I started to have a fit. I felt I was choking. He was going to call an ambulance but I indicated for him to call Vikki. I felt that Vikki could help me. Why? I did not know. My partner was so upset and nervous watching my body thrashing about on the bed. He called Vikki. It was in the middle of the night for her. She didn't get upset or even mention the time. She was there for me. Vikki talked me through the fit and, 30 minutes later, it was over. I was exhausted and slept peacefully the rest of the night. I have not had another fit since then. My nightmares and night terrors are gone.

   Six weeks after working with Vikki, I woke one morning and felt that could walk around my home with ease. I breathe easier and I know I am safe in my own home. Even my partner felt something had changed. He also noticed that the pressure on his head and shoulders had lifted.

   I carried on with LSL with both Vikki and Tom. I knew that there were more positive changes to come. After eight intense weeks working with Vikki, I could truly say that prior to LSL I was in hell and did not even realize it. Vikki helped pulled me out of this living nightmare. There were slight glimmers of real happy moments in the early weeks. The happier times are now more part of my daily life and the sad moments are getting a lot less.

Doing the interview for this story was not easy. It wasn't easy having to relive all that I have put behind me thanks to LSL. Now I want to help others understand that there is help out there. Even when you feel nothing can help you, LSL can.

The positive effects of LSL are immense. I recently have had two job interviews. I know that nine months ago I would have been composed enough to attend an interview, let alone have a job. The feedback from the interviewers were very positive and I could actually hear the good things about me.

LSL works in subtle ways. The changes in me have been gradual. My partner has seen the gradual positive change. He was skeptical at first but now he has even had sessions with Vikki.

I am not where I want to be with my life plan, yet. After all, I've only been working with Vikki for nine months. If I never made that initial visit to Tom and made the call to Vikki I would not have a life to live. So many ugly things have happened to my partner and myself. I have only given a brief outline here. We can only thank the sequence of events that led us to Tom and Vikki. They were, and still are here for me.

If you need help, support, or encouragement in your life, just make the call. There's nothing to lose and so much to gain. I am finding my confidence and now do not really care what others think about me. Even to my partner's amazement, I have forgiven my brother and family. LSL helped me to let go of my hatred. I am nervous about my future but at least I now have a future unlike before. Miracles happen around Vikki. Whatever brought me to Tom and Vikki was a true miracle and has saved my life.

Thank you Tom and Vikki

Maddy

Run Over by a Thought Train

Hi my name is Lee Duignan. I am a professional landscaper. I own my own business.

I have suffered from anxiety and panic attacks and self-confidence issues for many years. For as far back as I can remember I would overthink things. I worried about them. Whatever my thoughts were or whatever I was worried about consumed me. I thought about it always. I'd think about it when I drove. I'd think about it when I was at work. Because I overthought, stressed, and worried, I started suffering from headaches and stomach issues. I was drained and had lower back issues. I lived in a constant state of dread and hopelessness. I justified all my physical ailments by blaming my profession.

This is an example of how my thoughts go like an out-of-control training.

I remember back in my 20's I was in a relationship with a girl and I found out that she went to school with some people I knew. I asked her if she had dated any of them. I believed her when she told me no. However, I could not get the thoughts out of my head. On one level I believed her, but in my mind, the thoughts would play over and over again.

The negative belief was that I didn't want any of my girlfriends to have dated anybody I knew. I don't even know where that thought or belief came from but I believed it as fact. I would have the negative thoughts about her, about what she was doing, and who she knew. The thought train would run over me. It would consume every aspect of my mind. I would question myself about being with her, about if I was good enough, if she was comparing me, if she loved me, if I was worthy of her, if she was judging me, if she was lying, if I was pleasing her, and the list went on and so did the train. I would cause myself to have a panic attack. This is just one example. There are many negative trains in my mind and they ran constantly.

I have always been into my sports and going to the gym. I really wasn't getting the results I wanted. I got injured a lot. My lower back was getting worse. The pain was awful. I looked for a gym that had personal trainers. I found Winning Health Solutions.

I decided to go in and talk to someone. I talked to the owner and personal trainer, Tom Hibbert. Working with Tom was great. My body started to get in shape but there were still areas that needed improvement. Because of all of my injuries and pains, Tom suggested that I talk to a Lotus Seed Life (LSL) specialist. I trusted Tom and still do. I confided in Tom that I was suffering from terrible anxiety and panic attacks. He told me I should definitely talk to LSL.

I started working LSL specialist Vicki Wright. We did several sessions and with each session I felt better and better.

One day we did a session on addictions, that session changed my life. I had been addicted to all the negative thought trains. I was addicted to my anxiety attacks. I was addicted to dreading everything.

Another example of my addictions is that 3 to 4 weeks after doing the addiction session I was cleaning out my flat. I found a huge bag of headache tablets, nauseous tablets, sickness tablets, and all kind of medications. When I would go abroad I would buy extra medications because I didn't need a prescription for different tablets outside the UK. That way I would have the tablets in case I got sick at home. I had been taking sickness tablets constantly. I didn't even realize how many I was taking. When I found the large bag, most of the tablets were out of date. My girlfriend pointed out that I had not taken any medication tablets for over a year; ever since I started LSL. My mom, my girlfriend, my family members, my friends all told me I was addicted to medication tablets. I didn't pay any attention to them because none of them really knew how many I was taking or how often.

Looking back on it, I was also addicted to eating rubbish. I would go to the store to buy a paper and buy 10 candy bars, or 10 bags of crisps. Through LSL I also learned that I'm in control of what I put in my mouth. No one is making me eat rubbish. This one statement changed my eating habits, my weight and my strengths level. I am now lifting double what I was lifting a year ago.

With Tom as my trainer and Vicki as my mindset coach, I am now training to compete in my first novice strongman competition. I can confidently say that this goal is now a possibility.

Now for the other areas of my life: I am in a 10-year relationship with a wonderful lady. I go out and do things with other people. I have more confidence. I am relaxed around people. I know I am doing my best. I am healthier. I am pain free. I am worry free. I am medication-tablet free. I have a better outlook. I have more fun. I am playful, energized and on top of the world.

I believe everyone has to help themselves but LSL is there to help support you in your changes. The changes that LSL and I have made in my life are monumental. You, too, can make monumental changes.

Thank you, Tom, Vicki, and Vikki Fuadel.

Lee

Sometimes Life Hits You Upside the Head

I heard about Lotus Seed Life (LSL) long before I decided to give it a try. My ex (and now friend) told me about LSL and how I should do it. It would help my business, it would help me personally, it would help my general attitude and all the things that I was struggling with; that's what she kept telling me.

I kept putting it off because I didn't have a enough of a reason to do it. I kept thinking that things weren't that bad. I could handle it. I made light of my problems. I can put up with anything. I didn't take it seriously.

What really pushed me to make the call was that my flatmate and I got our house broke into and we were attacked in the middle of the night. That incident really pushed me to see I couldn't handle it. I couldn't cope with it. I couldn't make light of it. My friend told me that this was a sign that I needed to do something so I made the call.

I called 12 hours after the incident. I was sitting back in my house where I had been violated. I had a stitches from the gash on my head where I had been attacked. I was truly freaking out. I had my first session. After that session I immediately felt that everything was going to be okay. I felt like I could deal with it. I felt that I had the strength. This sounds kind of weird, but I felt that I was partially glad that it happened to me because, out of all of my friends and family, I could handle it because of my strength. It had an immediate impact on me. I had another session 24 hours after that which really showed me how strong I am. If I can handle this then "wow" what else can I handle?

My old defensive mechanism was to joke about things and make light of things. I couldn't get this traumatic incident out of my head. I couldn't joke it away. LSL helped me to admit that this did happen and how traumatic it was. It helped me take steps to get over it. I think it's less productive and worse, in the long run, to make light of it or joke about it. Some things you can't joke away. Acknowledging the incident and facing the fears around it helped me to get through it way quicker and easier. LSL was an altering of my mindset in order to get me through dealing with this trauma.

It's not just that incident that LSL has helped me with. LSL has taught me how to deal with the day-to-day things head on. I now face everything, in my personal life, in my business life and in every aspect.

As a musician, I am in the spotlight. I used to worry all the time about people judging me. What are they thinking about me? Are they enjoying the show? Do they like my music? Because of LSL, other people's opinions and judgments don't affect me anymore. I now focus on what I'm doing, being my best, and being proud of what I am doing. Sometimes I think that I take a step backwards when one of my insecurities comes up but I know that in the next session I will address whatever that insecurity is. It's not about being perfect, it's about being aware of these things so that I know how to deal with them.

I believe that LSL has also helped me in building friendships and relationships with people that, in the past, I would not have had the guts to engage with, let alone have a friendship. I have often felt like an introver; not wanting to deal with people. But after sessions, I now feel that I meet people easily. I recently went to Canada and met lots of really cool people. I know I had a positive impact on them. More importantly, they had a positive impact on me. All this is dueto LSL sessions. The LSL sessions taught me to value me for who I am and to value all the people that I meet for who they are.

My advice to anyone would be give it a go don't let it get bad enough to where someone at the break in your house and hit you over the head to try it. No one ever has a problem going to the gym and working out and taking care of their bodies. Well, LSL is the tool to take care of your mindset. It really is liberating to know that you can handle anything that comes at you. Even if it's just a small annoyance, enough to stress you out, is more stress than anyone needs in their life. Don't make light of any anomaly in your life. If there's something that feels wrong, it needs addressing; it needs facing head-on and LSL is the way to do it. LSL helped me develop my own mind in order to deal with life.

Just give it a go.

Steve

Going to the Chapel

I would first like to say thank you for helping me over the last 10 months. Together, we have achieved incredible results for such a short period of time. I feel like my life is on track. I now approach many things with a whole new mindset.

I used to have a problem making cold calls. Cold calling was a big part of my job. I didn't have the confidence. Calling was always very traumatic for me. It would often take me several hours to get in the right state of mind. I'd have to physically and mentally prepare myself to pick up the phone to make a call. After working with Lotus Seed Life (LSL), I have the confidence that I can make the calls and it only takes me a few minutes of preparation to get into the right mindset to pick up the phone and call whoever I need to.

The second massive assistance that LSL provided me. I was to be able to attend my son's wedding. Let me backtrack a little bit. I had a lot of issues with my previous marriage. I didn't want anything to do with my ex to the point I was fully prepared avoid my son's wedding so that I would not have to deal with the drama around his dad and his dad's new wife.

After sorting out lots of issues to do with my previous marriage and the impact that it had on my kids, I was actually looking forward to the day and being at my son's wedding. The day was fantastic! I felt good. I looked good. I kept smiling. I actually enjoyed the entire day. I was in such a good place, thanks to LSL. I subsequently was able to help my kids deal with a couple of issues that arose for them with their dad.

Finally the other large thing you have helped me with, was to move to Wales. This move happened five years ahead of our plan.

In between those major events there have been loads and loads of smaller things that have been sorted out; accepting me, my relationships, dealing with tiredness, headaches, and other day-to-day challenges. Thank you for your love and support.

Vicki Wright has helped me transform my life in a number of ways including my relationships with my family, helping me move on with my life and letting go of the past. She has been instrumental in supporting and overcoming my fear of using the telephone with regards to cold calls. Vicki has supported me in being able to attend and thoroughly enjoy a family event that I would have otherwise not attended. Instead of feeling like life is not worth living I am thankful for each and every day and enjoy every bit of life now.

I can't thank you enough and I'm sure you will continue to sort things out for a lot of other people.

Bernadette

How I Rescued Myself

Once upon a time a young country girl moved to the city far away from her family to start a new life for herself. But the young girl was naïve and unbeknownst to her, many men thought they could take advantage of her and did. This young girl saw the good in everyone. When someone showed her kindness she showed them kindness back and couldn't see they were taking advantage of her. This young girl is me (Emma).

I bounced from one bad relationship to the next where my boyfriends were constantly taking advantage of me and taking me for granted. Then, one day, I thought I had found my Prince Charming. This man showed me so much love and care. I let him into my life after a very short time. He had nothing so I gave him everything. He encouraged me, pushed me to better myself and gave me guidance where I needed it. He supported me in everything. I truly thought he was doing it all for me. We were married and the guidance soon turned into manipulation. The encouragement and pushing me to better myself turned into controlling my every move. The support turned into exercises in what could do for him. As the years went on I felt like I didn't mean anything. I was constantly walking on eggshells. I felt like I didn't deserve anything. I was never good enough. Everything I did became about him. He was always looking to get the best for him, and I didn't matter.

As the years went on I started to physically work out. My character grew stronger. I grew confident in my abilities. As my confidence grew, his "support," "encouragement," and "guidance" lessened. I was starting to see the real him. At the time, my husband wanted me to be bigger, fatter and out of shape. He was always telling me I wasn't good enough. I was very self-conscious. I didn't feel good. I didn't look good. I was very unhappy.

To keep the peace, I started justifying his words and actions. *He doesn't mean it. He is only trying to be helpful.* When someone uses your words and actions against you, down deep you really know that something's wrong. I knew there was something fundamentally wrong with our relationship but I wasn't strong enough to do anything about it and things got worse. You could say that Prince Charming threw me into the dungeon of our castle and kept me locked there. I was trapped. I felt trapped. Try as I might, I couldn't break free. The walls were too high and the world was too scary. I tried to leave several times and every time I started to climb out, the wall seem to grow taller. I just couldn't see how to get over them. I had grown into the person he wanted; into the person I was when I was with him. I was scared of the world without him. For years, I believed everything he told me. He fed on my fears and made them bigger and more intense than reality. The more I worked out and got in shape, the worse things got.

While I was in the dungeon, things were looking pretty dark pretty dreary and pretty dreadful. A great thing happened. I discovered three mice. We became friends. I talked to the mice every week. My belief that I could be free was growing. The mice worked together to show me there was a way out. They showed me if I put my mind to it, and eliminated my fears, I could be free. I could be the person I wanted to be. These three mice showed me I didn't have to climb the castle walls because there was another way. All I needed was the right mindset to see that the door door had been unlocked the entire time. I had to be strong enough to push the door open. For all those years, my husband and my fears caused me to believe the door was locked and there was no getting out.

One day, I decided I was strong enough to push the door open and walk out. Well I pushed and pushed. The huge, heavy door opened and out I went. Outside the door was every obstacle I could imagine carefully put on my path by my husband. To entice and scare me back to him, and back to the safety of my bondage. I knew I had taken the first step, the most difficult step, and that no matter how hard the rest of the journey was I made the right decision.

Logistically, at this time, my husband and I were still living in the same house but in separate bedrooms. One day I talked to one of the mice. After doing a Lotus Seed Life (LSL) session my homework was to go out and buy myself a set of sheets. I really thought the mouse (Vicki), was crazy. But I did it. When I came home I went into what used to be our room together. I started bagging up things. My husband thought I was being nice and packing all this stuff for him. After all, everything's about him. But truly, I was getting rid of and letting go of everything that reminded me of my imprisoned years. I then made the bed with the new sheets. It was so liberating and freeing to claim that space as mine and only mine; to make that space my own safe peaceful haven. I was giving myself a fresh start. I felt like me, empowered me, strong me, a brand-new me, in my brand-new life. All of this came from one tiny act of buying new sheets.

With the help of the mice my belief in myself grew and I managed to step over each of the obstacles that have been put on my path. As I eliminated each of the obstacles I received more and more clarity. Things in my life started going right. Some of the obstacles disappeared on their own.

At moments, I had a few panic attacks and some setbacks but the three mice were with me all the way. They encouraged me to keep going or to find a different path, to believe in myself, to tackle one thing at a time and to believe I could do anything. The mice could see my potential. All I had to do was have the mindset and the right support; which I do. I now believe I can do anything.

Well this may have started out in a fairy tale style but this was my life. I cannot say enough about LSL and Tom Hibbert. The kind of support I have received seemed like a fairy tale at times. The three mice helped me more than they will ever know. The unconditional acceptance, empowerment, and the belief in me, that they continue to show me is truly unbelievable.

I would like to introduce you to my three mice friends, mouse # 1 is Tom Hibbert, mouse # 2 is Vikki Faudel, and mouse #3 is Vicki Wright.

I have so many stories about Tom and the LSL team I could fill a whole book. I will end the story here but I would like to share a couple of other ways that Tom Hibbert and LSL team have helped me.

Tom Hibbert of Winning Health Solutions was recommended to me for his work with injury rehabilitation and body composition. I started training with Tom. I felt better physically. I mentioned to Tom that I hadn't had a period in quite a while. Tom told me I needed to talk to Vikki, the founder of LSL. At the time I thought it was very strange, but I trust Tom.

I called Vikki. In our initial interview, Vikki told me that my periods had stopped because of what was happening in my relationship. She told me that once I had sorted my relationship out my period would come back. She told me that I was reserved and felt as if my spirit had been broken. She told me that I was trapped and had nowhere to go but up. She believed I could do anything.

It was very hard to believe a woman that didn't know me, didn't know anything about me, but was on the other end of the phone 1,000 miles could be so spot on. My period returned less than a week after telling my husband I wanted a divorce.

Vikki told me that doing sessions with LSL would change my mindset. I decided to take a chance. I started working with LSL. Vikki had me start doing sessions with one of her specialists, Vicki Wright. We worked once a week. I would call Vicki and talk to her about what was going on. Then we would do a session. With each session I felt more and more powerful, respected, deserving, worthy of the very best. I was making the right decisions for me.

Working with Tom gave me the courage to set a goal of getting up on stage in a bodybuilding competition. In my very first competition I placed in the top five in the UK. This led me to my next competition where I placed 5th in the overall competition and 1st in the body transformation competition. I then qualified to compete in the world championship where I placed 9th out of 530 contestants in my 1st year! After receiving this kind of recognition and accolades, I believe I can achieve anything I set my mind to.

LSL has also helped me with my nutrition by getting me over my sugar fixation and bingeing. This is very important for my sport of competing with the best of the best in World Beauty Fitness and Fashion (WBFF), and achieving my goal of winning the world championships.

One of the other correlations that I want to mention is that I have learned that all of my aches and pains stem from something emotional that's going on in my life. If I'm stressed over something or worried about something I will have a physical reaction. I will have a pain somewhere in my body. My pain always coincides with something going on in my life. Once I do a session and figure out what my issue is, the pain is gone.

Through all of this my, biggest life lesson has been to have confidence in myself and believe in myself. Before Tom and before LSL I didn't know what it meant to believe in myself or what that felt like. Now I can genuinely say I believe in me and I am confident. When I'm on stage, my stage presence exudes all of my genuine beliefs. I compete against me. You can have the best body in the world but if you're not coming across in the right way on stage you'll get marked down. The judges can see my sincere confidence and belief in myself.

My advice to anyone and everyone is that if you heard of, or been led to LSL, there is a reason. Trust it, trust the team, trust your intuition, make the most out of every session. Do what they tell you to do. Believe that LSL will help you. The way to get the most out of every session is to share everything with your practitioner. When you start talking to your specialist there's a fear of telling them everything, a fear of being judged, a fear of their reaction, in a fear that it will be used against you. Share those fears with them. These individuals have been trained by the best. They have gone through the entire process themselves. This means they have done every session in the book. They have become the most loving, caring, understanding, and empathetic people you will ever meet. Trust them.

When I started with Tom and LSL I was VERY skeptical. I didn't understand what I was going to get out of it. Now my life is totally changed, better than I could've ever imagined. I don't know how to thank all of you. I could not have done any of this without Tom or LSL.

Thank you Tom Hibbert, Vicki Wright, and Vikki Faudel.

Emma

Fly in the Ointment

Well to start with I was part of a group called Ladies for Networking and, as part of that group, I won a free Lotus Seed Life (LSL) session. I had no idea what it was about or what it could do for me.

I had a good life and I had a successful business, but I did have one fly in the ointment that caused me a lot of stress, a lot of time, and I didn't know how to deal with it, handle it or what to do about it. I knew this fly in the ointment was holding me back. I was working in networking marketing. I had a problem with a person that was in my up line, we will call her Jackie. With me being in her downline and being successful she obviously noticed a lot of my activity. She contacted me to set up weekly calls. We became colleagues. These phone calls were to be a forum to bouncing ideas off each other, to get inspiration, to continue to build our own businesses.

However, she started calling me at random times, three to four times a week. They soon became a two to three dictatorial conversation. She was bigoted towards other people in the company. She manipulated the conversation so that I could not get a word in edgewise. I absolutely love the company. I dreaded every call with her, but, being a proper English woman, I would not tell her that she was taking up my time, that I needed to run my business or how I felt about what she was saying. So this was the fly in the ointment that I went to LSL for.

After my third or fourth session, I began to get very brave and told Jackie that I couldn't talk when she called. I would then arrange a time to talk for a specific amount of time. I also found the courage to keep it to the specific time that I had allotted for the call. LSL gave me the coping skills for this fly in the ointment.

Lotus seed life has had a knock on effect. It has made me think more deeply. It has made me more proactive rather than reactive. I'm a lot calmer in every situation. I am now more my own person with choices and direction.

My advice to anyone is, no matter how skeptical you are, give it a go. Until you try LSL you will not know how powerful, life-affirming, and life-changing it really is.

Thank you very much,
GEM

Finding my Pieces

I'm sure that many of you will be able to relate to my story. My life was quite complicated. I made bad choices. I attracted negative people. I had people around me who would take from me and who manipulated me to do what they wanted. The people around me would just take take take to benefit them. I was constantly drained physically and mentally and emotionally. I would do for people but when I needed something they were nowhere to be found. I didn't have any time for myself or to grow my business. I was frustrated, tired, exhausted, and generally feeling very negative about everything. I was in a relationship that was filled with lies and deceitfulness.

My dad suggested that I work with Lotus Seed Life (LSL). I was very skeptical but if thought *if it'll make my dad happy okay, I'll try it*. When I first had my first session I felt very very weird. I wondered what I was getting into.

The LSL really made me think; it made me think about what I was doing in life. It made me think about what other people were doing to me and what I was putting up with from other people. Things became easier after about two months. I was calm her and didn't get as worked up with people and their drama. I think that the changes for me were little ones that kept building on one another until one day I had the strength, the courage's, and the empowerment to say enough is enough.

During my life, everybody took little pieces of me and

pretty soon I didn't have anything left of me. I regained those pieces doing LSL. With every session I got back more of me. I totally believe that if I had not done the LSL sessions that I would still be in a detrimental relationship and everything in life would be more difficult.

The sessions that made the most impact on me dealt with respect and responsibility. The sessions dealing with respect taught me how to respect myself. They taught me that I was worth respecting. Those sessions also taught me not to put any weight or importance in other people's opinions. Those sessions were very impactful for me. The sessions on responsibility taught me that I don't have to be responsible for making other people happy. It's not my responsibility to look after everybody else, my responsibility is to me. These sessions changed my life.

I have met a wonderful man. We are getting married later in the year. My business is growing. I am attracting in positive lovely people.

It is all because I am thinking right, and if I'm thinking right, good things happen. People showed me more respect because I was taking care of myself instead of making everyone else more important than me.

My overall view of LSL is that it fixed me. It gave me back to me. My advice to others is that no matter how weird you think it is, what do you have the lose. Give it a go!

It is absolutely life-changing. It changed the way I think, the way I act, and the people I attract. I am so grateful for LSL and Gill Wright, for being the specialist she is and introducing me to LSL.

Thank you,
Nicki Whaites

My Onion

Working with Lotus Seed Life has helped me work out some serious stuff. It is all the deep stuff that I didn't even know I had buried along the way. Getting rid of my destructive habits has been the biggest transition for me personally. Gill Wright has been more than just my guide through this journey, peeling away at the onion, as I call it. She challenged me. She help me see things in a completely different perspective. She is brilliant at knowing exactly what I need to work on. Her intuition astounds me at times. I find myself thinking "how did she know that?" Her intuition, her perception, is what makes her a naturally gifted specialist.

Saying that LSL has changed my life sounds like a cliché, however it has. I would encourage everyone to invest in themselves first and foremost before thinking of making any other financial investments anywhere else. This will be the most powerful investment you will make and you will find everything else will naturally fall into place as a result. I have cleared a lot of stuff, my business has grown, I have lost weight, I have let go of my destructive relationships, but the best gift of all is I look in the mirror and I now love and respect who I have become as a result of LSL letting go.

Thank you, Gill and Vikki, I always refer to you two ladies as my it Lotus Seed Life Angels.

Mandy Burger,

The Importance of Peanut Butter

I don't truly know how to thank Lotus Seed Life (LSL), Vikki Faudel and Vicki Wright. The changes to my mindset, to my beliefs, to my knowledge, to my abilities and to my life have been immense. All I can do is simply say "THANK YOU".

I am smarter, wiser, a better parent, a great wife and a wonderful person. I married a wonderful man. His name is Phil. Phil is so kind, caring, and generous. The relationship that I have with him is a partnership and is phenomenal. I'm completely respected. I am treated like I matter. I am treated like I make a difference. He loves and respects my children. My children love and respect him. LSL has taught me to be a more understanding and patient parent. I have three amazing children. I can now accept how gifted and talented they are. I now know how talented and intuitive I am. I believe I can do anything that I put my mind to. I believe in me. I believe in each one of them. I finally believe it's okay to be me. I believe that I am safe to being me. I am secure in all I have to give. I can do anything. For the first time in my life, I love me. Loving me makes it possible to love others even more. All of this is because of LSL.

My life was not always been like this.

In my younger years, my biological father was very moody and beat my mother. I remember him beating her head against the cupboard door one time. We used to walk around on eggshells when he was around. Once they split up he was very sporadic in seeing us kids. I remember standing outside on the porch for hours waiting for him to come to see us but he never came.

My mom then married another man. I took to him very quickly because I was so desperate for a father-daughter bond. I was nine when he started sexually molested me. It started out by him coming into the bathroom when I was taking baths. Then he started touching me. I was the prime target because I was affectionate and I would do anything for him. I didn't know it was wrong.

He would make us clean everything. Every day we had to do the dinner dishes. If they weren't good enough he'd make us do them again. Once a week he would take everything out of the all the cupboards and make us wash everything. We cleaned everything. He had his own cupboard in the kitchen that was locked. We were not allowed to have any of his food. We ate beans and toasts for a whole year. To this day I gag at the thought of beans and toast. I remember one time my stepdad locked himself in the garage with my sister and beat her with a bamboo stick. It was horrific. My mom knew what was going on but didn't do anything to stop it. My mom would often talk us into doing things that she knew were wrong. She would go tell him and get us into trouble. I learned quickly not to trust her. She would constantly trick us. If he beat us, he didn't beat her. I was about 15, when he beat my mom up really bad and we moved to a different town.

When I was 15, I got into a relationship with a guy who was totally into abuse and violence. But I thought that's how relationships were. I didn't know any difference. I had my first child when I was 17. We got married when I was 20. I married him because I was so paranoid of what society would think and say about me for having a child. I was getting ready to leave him when I got pregnant with our 2nd daughter. He was beating me constantly. He tried to strangle me a few times. He threatened me all the time. I had no confidence and no friends he controlled everything. He told me what I could eat and couldn't eat. When my 2nd daughter was one year old I went on empowerment course for women. I left that relationship.

I got into a string of bad relationships one after another. I kept attracting the same kind of person, the abuser, over and over. I couldn't stop no matter how much therapy or self-development I went to or tried. I couldn't stop the pattern.

I went to the University and I met a man and I got pregnant with my 3rd child. At the time, I thought this man was different. But I was wrong. He was just as bad if not worse than the others.

I went to the University and in my 2nd year my essay scores were at 38% which is just barely scraping by. After taking some tests at the University I was diagnosed with having dyslexia. I was in a gap year from the University to give birth to a 3rd child and to care for my other children. I started a network marketing group. I didn't really want to but I had to do something. I was easily manipulated. I was very sad. I was depressed. I was stressed out to the max. I had low self-confidence. I was constantly beating myself up about my degree. I was dreading going back to the University. I was at a very low point in my life.

When I first started my psychotherapy I would sit in silence for long periods of time and wait for the psychotherapist to say something. With every question that I would ask they didn't have a response. I was often frightened and bored. I believe that all my therapists were judging me and that they were without fault.

I went on empowerment course for women and I was introduced to a woman with connections to LSL. This wonderful lady introduced me to Lotus Seed Life.

I gave Vikki Faudel a call one day. That call changed my life. I talked to her and felt like she was real and genuine. She acknowledged me and listened to me. She talked to me about starting sessions with one of her specialists also named Vicki.

After 3 months of doing sessions I did the session on abuse. That session gave me the courage to leave my son's father. It gave me the courage to move away from my family and all the abusers in my life.

I know this sounds like a small incident but those of you who have ever been in an abusive relationship will understand. The first time I went to the grocery store after being out of the abusive cycle it dawned on me that I could actually buy what I wanted. From my stepfather to my most recent ex I could not have butter because I was not worth it. But now I can eat all the butter I want and I love it.

I moved closer to the University and finished my program. After 6 months of doing LSL, my essay grade went to a 62 which is pretty amazing. I didn't believe I could ever get my degree because I was too stupid. After all, I had been told I was stupid all of my life. I never thought I could do so well at anything. I stopped questioning myself. I stopped holding myself back. I stopped beating myself up. All of my grades improved. For my dissertation I wrote over 40,000 words which is totally amazing for someone so "stupid." My professor told me I should have it published. I graduated with my psychology degree.

Even with my degree I know that psychologists and psychiatrists and psychotherapist don't work as well as LSL. I remember being in a lecture with a guest speaker on dementia. The professor talked about how the tests they used to assess dementia don't work. When I asked him why we're still using the test even though they don't work, his answer was "because that's the way it's always been done." As a student, I felt that was really a rubbish answer. I felt I couldn't talk to him about it as he was in the mindset that we can't change the way things are, we accept them as is. After all, he was the professor and always right.

In my past, every time I talk to a therapist or a psychologist or psychiatrist or my professors I would ask questions and no one would have answers. There were holes in everything. I have a great knack for finding the holes. The holes (as I call them) are when things don't add up or don't work. LSL doesn't have any holes.

After about a year I received an email from LSL. The email was an invitation to go to a retreat in Colorado. I thought it was going to be a glorified holiday and I wasn't sure I wanted to go. I thought we'd be sitting around and taking yoga classes and being taught by a guru. I figured we'd be talked to by special speakers. I didn't really want to participate. Boy, was I wrong!

I traveled to the Colorado retreat with my specialist, Vicki. Vikki and her husband, Nate, welcomed us into their home. It was like one big happy family. It was a community of everybody working together for a common goal whether the goal was doing the dishes or cooking together. I felt like I was part of a family. The retreat taught me a lot but I was never once in a classroom.

I remember one of the first few days being in the kitchen with Vikki making dessert. As I was mixing the ingredients with peanut butter I was thinking *I'll put some peanut butter on Vikki's face! What will she think? What will she do?* Well I did it! I put peanut butter on her nose. It was a pivotal moment for me. I knew then that I was safe to be myself. I can be playful and mischievous. I knew then that I could open up to this woman. I also knew that it was okay to believe this woman. I knew then I was never going to not listen to what this woman had to say again. She didn't scold me. She didn't judge me. She tried to put peanut butter on my face. She totally respected my wishes and my boundaries. It was a great experience. You don't normally cross boundaries with your therapist or your psychologist or psychiatrist and sometimes not even your own mother. But with Vikki, I could be playful and still have the utmost respect and admiration because she let me be me. She accepted me for who I was and had no expectations of me

On this retreat, I also learned that my mother was very conditional. When she gave a gift it was because it was good for her. She never gave a real choice, it was always her choice. On the retreat, and through the sessions, I learned I have the freedom to feel what I want to feel; the freedom to choose what I want.

The retreat was very insightful, empowering, and challenging. Being with a group of people with so many different backgrounds, different personalities, different cultures can sometimes be tough but not on the Colorado retreat. Sometimes you get nudged out of your comfort zone. But even being out of my comfort zone, I still felt safe. I had never trusted anyone. I now not only trust myself, I trust my instincts, and my feelings. I also trust Vikki, Nate, and Vicki.

My advice is to start! When you start, keep going because you won't recognize that you've ever lived a different way. But you will be more yourself and be secure in who you are. You will have new freedom. You will be proud of who you are and what you do.

I highly recommend LSL.

Rachel Wharf

Receiving

My journey through life had made me aware of so many different kinds of holistic therapies and treatments. I was into the crystals and aromatherapy and had tried several different types of therapies. I wasn't happy. I was a bit in the doldrums. You could say I had a negative mindset. I was down on myself. I was looking for something more and, as I looked for more, I went into a networking meeting which I dislike it immensely. That's where I met Gill Wright who talked about Lotus Seed Life (LSL) and how it made changes in people's lives. As we were sitting talking over coffee I decided to give it a try. The more Gill and I talked, the more I began to identify with what she was saying and trusting that she could help me make the changes in my patterns that I wanted. I started doing sessions and I started to notice small changes; changes in my relationship with my partner and changes in my confidence level. I was becoming more and more confident and, as my confidence grew, I was able to say things that I'd always wanted to say and was able to ask for what I wanted.

My relationship with my mother was one that was unhealthy for me. As I grew older, I kept my mother at a distance. At the time, I was trying to balance the unhealthy extremes of being too close to my mother and of being too distant for my mother. With Gill's help, I was able to maintain who I am in the relationship with my mom to the point that now that we have a very honest open and loving relationship. I never anticipated was even a possibility.

The session that had the most impact on me was one on gratitude and, through that session, I learned that giving is important but also receiving with gratitude is just as important. That concept really resonated with me more than any other session. I was able to learn to really receive and receive graciously. That session had homework for me. I was to go out and do something for someone without claiming any credit for it. It gave me such a good feeling that I still do it today. I will buy someone a coffee or I will do something nice for others without any acknowledgment or just do it anonymously which makes me feel good all over.

One of the long-term changes that has taken place because LSL is that I now realize that other people and their attitudes or their state of mind does not affect me. It does not affect my mood, my mindset or any part of my life. If my partner is not feeling a hundred percent because of his health issues or if my friend is not positive and just wants to stay in her negativity, I know I can remain positive and true to myself. I am the one in charge of my mindset and in charge of what kind of day, week, or month I have.

Lotus seed life, Gill Wright, and Vikki Faudel have had such a massive positive impact on my life that I cannot recommend it highly enough to anyone.

Thank you,
Lisa B

The Blind Musician

I was born in Marshall, Minnesota. For the first 18 months of my life my parents and my doctors thought I had cerebral palsy because everything, from speech development to mobility, was dramatically delayed. It wasn't until my babysitter asked my parents, "Have you gotten Steve's eyes checked?" that they learned that I had eye problems. I was born with RP (retinitis pigmentosa) and Cone/Rod Dystrophy. Even with corrected vision, I was legally blind.

Nevertheless, I grew up in a great household with two loving and hard-working parents. My father was a preacher and my mother was a teacher. Life was pretty good, but like any parent-child relationship, we definitely didn't see eye-to-eye (pardon the pun) on everything. I knew the love was there. I learned what compassion, principle and effort meant. At home I was taught the violin and piano from an early age. Later, when we moved to Fort Collins, Colorado, I got to grow up spending summers at my father's Lutheran camp surrounded by progressive ideas and fresh air. Add in some great friends (like Nate Faudel), first loves, piano concerts and being the frontman for a progressive metal band, and you've got a pretty fantastic upbringing.

But as much as I pretended not to have a disability - because I wanted to be like everyone else (and I wanted girls to like me) - there were still many challenges I had to face. From learning music differently via the Suzuki method, to adjusting how I would tackle ever-increasing work loads at school each year, life could be difficult.

It wasn't until I went to college in Minnesota that I really learned how my disability was going to affect my education. I might have been able to read 40% of the material, but I barely escaped with a BA in Social Studies Education. During this time, music - writing original piano music and orchestral pieces on my Roland synthesizer workstation - gave me solace and inspiration to continue on and become a world-famous concert pianist. (The degree was just a back up...or so I kept telling myself.) I also left with an army of friends for life.

Things were still a bit tough for me regarding my disability but I have always been able to adapt to challenges. It's how I got as far as I did. It wasn't until a family trip to Europe at the end of my college tenure that things took a turn. While shopping in Geneva, I started noticing things - or not noticing things - in my field of vision. I thought little of it until we got home and I went to see my opthamologist Dr. Alexander; she dropped a bombshell. She told me that I had Macular Degenration. I was going to continue losing my center sight until maybe (hopefully) it plateaued, or, well, bottomed out.

This diagnosis destroyed me. Not only did I believe I was going to lose most of my sight, but questioned how would it affect me playing the piano, see friends (literally) and them see me (socially). Would I become a reclusive pariah? Yes, it sounds a touch histrionic, but this, in fact, did happen. At first, I ignored the developing questions I had about my sight and how I would continue to have to adjust to a disease that would relentlessly strip the world away from me. I became more depressed. Depression is insidious. Over the next few years I tended to go out less, see friends less often, drink more (way more), binge-watch tv, date less, stop working out and ultimately give up on music altogether.

I didn't write a song for five years.

During my - or what my musical hero Serge Rachmaninoff called his - "blue period," I got involved with a brilliant and beautiful woman. She was pretty much my dream girl. I honestly didn't know how we ended up together but we did. The honeymoon phase was exquisite. Although there were many things to love about her, we both began to learn about the things that weren't so great about the other person - and boy did we learn...

We were together for several years before we decided to move in together, and that's where things really fell apart. Months after the move, we broke up. We were both devastated. But as much as the temptation mounted for us to get back together, I fundamentally knew that it was not a good idea. Already being depressed about my diminishing sight-loss (little did I understand how much), and not utilizing the natural processing power of music to help me, I spun out of control. The world became an abysmal liquor-infused borderline suicidal place.

Then, out of the blue (and on my ex's birthday of all days), I received a phone call from my long-lost dear childhood friend, Nate. We got to talking about life. He more or less listened while I complained a lot. Then over the following few months, we continued to talk and he told me about what he and his wife, Vikki, were doing; he told me about Lotus Seed Life (LSL). I was skeptical. Where were their Master's degrees and Ph.D.'s? Where did they practice? It didn't make a whole lot of sense to me, but Nate persisted; he knew LSL could and would help me. I am glad he did. LSL introduced me to Gill Wright, who would become my specialist for the next couple years. Gill was great; she was kind, sweet, thoughtful - and that attractive British accent sure helped, too. She was a consummate professional and I understood very quickly how much she cared about me and my well-being.

Although the sessions with Gill seemed to help, I wasn't

entirely convinced. Nate then offered to host me in their home for as long as it took to help me get my life back on track. I loved and respected Nate (still do). Although I wasn't sure how this LSL thing was going to go, I did understand that I needed a significant and drastic change in my lifestyle. So, on my birthday, after a session with Gill, I went for it. I moved across the country and into Vikki and Nate's home with their two brilliant and charming daughters in Highlands Ranch, Colorado.

Their home became an emotional and intellectual chrysalis for me. Living in a place with people who, daily, strived to make their lives and the lives of others better through LSL, was transformative. Having consistent sessions with Gill, intellectually sparring with Nate as we hiked the Rocky Mountains, emotional conversations with Vikki, and the best home-cooked meals provided the support and fuel for me to put in the hard work and make the changes I knew I needed to make.

Within weeks, I began playing the piano again and started writing new music. I got a gym membership and, nightly, would walk the mile-and-a-half (two-and-a-half kilometers) to work out and walk back feeling revitalized. Each day, I would wash, rinse and repeat. I lived the Lotus Seed Life.

Later that year, I put out my third solo piano album,"Labreya." Then, through rebuilding friendships (because I had the desire reborn within me), I reached out to my college friend Heather. With her and her husband's help, I got the tools to begin learning how to write music for media. I ingested countless hours of videos, tutorials, educational courses and masterclasses. Slowly, I learned to understand the language of music in film and how it supports the story.

Later that year, I had some of my music placed in a short film that screened at the Cannes Film Festival. A few months after that, I got to write a few pieces of music for a Christmas film.

Then, the director liked the music so much that he asked me to compose the music for the entire movie. This movie, *Santa's Boot Camp*, has now been released through Sony Pictures Home Entertainment. My score was also nominated for an award and the Love International Film Festival in Los Angeles.

I have now worked with actors from *The Hunger Games, Oceans Eleven, The Dark Knight, The Walking Dead*, and Emmy-Award winning editors, and directors from L.A. to Atlanta, Luxembourg and Italy. With new projects in the works and my own designs on programs to assist other people with disabilities find their voices through music, the future looks good.

Lotus Seed Life, the Faudel Family, a positive environment and a whole lot of hard work has led to a life I have always wanted. But with all things worth having, the work to better one's self must always and forever continue...

Steve Letnes

Conclusion

We all exist together, in the same world, with the same obstacles and challenges and with the same goals. We want to learn how live gracefully and get the very most out of the few years we have on this planet. We want to look back on our lives and know we made some sort of a difference and left the world a little better than we found it. This is an invitation to see what accessing your inner purpose and drive can do for you. Everyone has different skills, abilities, and potential. Everyone has a unique purpose and unlimited potential. This book is a book of explorers who have gone before you and now invite you to join them in this previously uncharted area of personal excellence and internal upward mobility.

Our pasts shape who we are today. Who we are today shapes our tomorrow. A few select people at any given moment in history make the leap beyond what was prescribed for them by the cultural expectations around them. This is one of those opportunities to leave all expectations behind and bloom into more than was ever thought "realistic." This is your chance to live the Lotus Seed Life.

More information can be found at www.LotusSeedLife.com or by calling 0203 371 7381 in the UK or (303) 995-2225 in the US.

If you would like your story featured in a future volume of a book like this please submit your story (500-3,000 words) to us. This invitation does not guarantee a date of publication.